Multinational Workplaces: War of Culturally Seasoned Minds

Vijesh Jain & Susana Costa e Silva

ISBN-10: 1518889832
ISBN-13: 978-1518889837

DEDICATION

This book is dedicated to several collaborators from around the world, who are actively involved in CFC research project and who voluntarily provided data and inputs to draw useful inferences for the contents of this book.

CONTENTS

ACKNOWLEDGMENTS

No research based text can be created without the unconditional support and guidance of mentors who have a belief in author's approach, enquiry, expertise, skills, potential and ideas. I am thankful for the passionate mentorship by *Dr. Rahul Singh, Dr. Arun Sahai, Dr. Deepak Tandon, Prof. Navneet Saxena, Dr. Raghuvendra Dwivedi, Dr. Mukesh Porwal, Dr. B.S. Hothi, Prof. A. R. Mishra* and others, who provided immense support and inputs to make this research based book meaningful and accurate. It is because of their spontaneous efforts and eagerness to be part of the social innovation which this book signifies, that it will be able to draw attention of the readers to a new perspective to intercultural comfort phenomenon in multicultural & multinational workplaces. A special acknowledgment deserves attention to the contribution of *Ms. Juliana Bernhofer* from *Università Ca' Foscari di Venezia, Italy* who shared one of the important sets of countries based primary data for the multinational studies done for writing this book.

PREFACE

The origin of this book is linked to an ongoing global research project, popularly named as CFC research, where the authors of the book are actively involved. The aim of the research is to study the phenomenon of implicit variation of tendency of different national cultures to feel comfortable or not feel so comfortable with the persons of other cultures.

This book however discusses the concept in the context of multinational workplaces and multicultural business environment. This book is a sincere attempt to study the level of comfort of the team members having local cultural background with the other members of different national origins. The book refers to this phenomenon as 'comfort with foreign cultures' or simply CFC. The book proposes that due to the cultural seasoning of the team members in multinational workplaces resulting from their unique cultural backgrounds they may or may not be comfortable with colleagues with foreign origins. This book assumes significance also due to the fact that more and more multinational enterprises (MNEs) are finding workplace diversity as a key driver to growth and to deriving of competitive advantage in fiercely competitive global business environment. The phenomenon of CFC has been studied in this context and clubbed with other similar studies done by other modern social scientists. Additionally the related concepts of cross cultural understanding have been included in this book to make the reading more valuable for the readers.

INTRODUCTION

Multicultural workplaces in multinational enterprises (MNEs) have been found to be the providers of the best team performances. Most multinational firms focus on strategies to bring cultural diversity at workplaces to improve performance. However, cultural diversity in multinational workplaces also poses new challenges, especially relating to friction and discomfort between team members having diverse cultural backgrounds in terms of uneasiness to work with; differences in perception about issues; differences in values and ethics; etc. This situation calls for management of multicultural workforce by the team managers in such ways as to reduce such friction or discomfort. The aim should be to improve 'interpersonal comfort' among multicultural team members. In order to achieve this effectively and to smoothly face day to day cultural glitches of managing such teams, it may be helpful to understand the structure of 'cross cultural comfort' among team members and also to identify the variables influencing such comfort, particularly the level of comfort of local cultures with foreign cultures (CFC) at workplaces. This 'level of CFC' in the book primarily refers to the 'relative ease and positivity of working among different cultural groups in international teams' specifically between members of local cultures and of foreign cultures. Such ease of working and positivity is likely to originate or be influenced by several implicit factors and dimensions which may vary among team members having different cultural backgrounds.

Therefore, this book focuses on understanding this variation in 'level of comfort' of local dominant cultural groups with other foreign cultural groups in multinational workplaces. The book also refers to a set of studies done by the authors of the book, to identify the role of different observed and latent variables having a significant bearing on the variation of 'level of CFC. These studies had also identified a few important and logical 'control variables' which may significantly control this variation. Authors also studied the significance and nature of the impact of these 'control variables' on 'level of CFC' and have described them in this book. Impacts of these control variables such as country of residence, city of residence, income group, age group, education level and gender have been discussed. However 'country' had been treated in this book as the chief control variable and has been discussed in more detail.

The book starts by describing theoretical foundations of the cross cultural management, multinational workplaces, global cultures, workplace cultural management and similar topics. Latest concepts of cross cultural management, management of multicultural teams, dealing with people's issues and others have been discussed in detail. The importance and process of effective leadership for inspiring multicultural teams have also been highlighted. A path of understanding world cultures has been discussed which can be very helpful for international team managers to understand the cultural ethos and lifestyles of employees with diverse cultural backgrounds. Methods of understanding of cultural differences through the concepts of cultural dimensions have been described too.

Later in the book, studies done by the authors for the primary theme of this book and their results are described. The first study is a preliminary study and relates to devising of a theoretical framework of 'level of comfort' of local cultures with foreign cultures (CFC) using a plethora of published information available for a set of identified countries. In order to further confirm findings of this study and to identify the specific observed and latent factors or variables affecting the intragroup comfort level, two primary data based studies were also done and are described in this book. First was a 'pilot study' and the second was a 'comprehensive study' on a two sets of selected countries. The pilot study was done based on responses from 9 countries, namely, *US, India, China, Brazil, Portugal, Kenya, Sweden, U.K.* and *Italy*. Later, a comprehensive study was done with a larger set of samples of responses from *India, Italy* and *Portugal*. The survey instrument helped identify latent variables affecting such 'level of CFC' in work teams at MNEs. In the later part of the book, a research done by the authors to study the concepts from country to country perspective, has also been described, which tried to identify the nature and significance of 'level of CFC' in the context of intercultural behavior between local dominant culture vis-a-vis other team members coming from specific cultural background i.e. CFC among 'country pairs'.

Finally results and observations from these studies have been analyzed and interpreted at the end of this book. Studies done by the authors and described in this book clearly indicate a variation of level of CFC from country to country, both in terms of the reaction of the locals to foreigners in general and towards specific country. Studies found it important to understand this variation deeply by the industry leaders and managers. The book also discusses the concepts of cross cultural management and how the inferences from these studies are useful for industry persons, students and trainers.

1. CROSS CULTURAL MANAGEMENT AT MULTICULTURAL WORKPLACES: AN INSIGHT

Due to globalization and increased international migration of people around the world, multiculturalism has become an inevitable reality. In such an environment, professionals working in multicultural, international project teams, face several cultural glitches and challenges which can have a bearing on the success or failures. It has been found that cross-cultural skills and foreign language competencies have become among important elements of modern job profiles[1]. Yet multiculturalism in international as well as national teams in large organizations and multinational enterprises (MNEs) pose great challenges for team leaders and managers. Discussions in following paragraphs relate to effective management of modern international project teams in global firms.

Diversity and multiculturalism in global companies

Formation of multicultural teams has become a strategic decision for global firms around the world. Contemporary international management literature has reported that the management of multicultural teams is an important aspect of human resources management. Multicultural teams are deployed because they are perceived to out-perform monoculture teams, especially when performance requires multiple skills and judgment. This is normally the case in most international projects in multinational enterprises (MNEs)[2]. Therefore, greater knowledge has been generated in the past to understand the key variables that lead to international project success. Still there is need for increased research efforts in understanding influential factors that affect multicultural project team performance. (*See exhibit 1.1 – Diversity in American Companies, in box below*)

Exhibit 1.1

Diversity in American Companies

Most companies, small or big in *America* recognize the advantages of diversity at the workplace. With proper management of diversity and integrating the persons from diverse background, companies become much stronger. In today's environment, as more and more companies are going global and interacting with different cultures, maintaining diversity at workplaces has become an integral part of the business plan. Most American companies reported from their own experience the following advantages of diversity at workplaces.

- Increase in creativity
- Increase in productivity
- Benefits of new attitudes
- Language Skills
- Better understanding of where *America* fits in global playfield
- Emergence of new processes

The list of what world's best companies like - *Cisco, Deloitte, General Mills, IBM and Procter & Gamble* do to encourage a welcoming atmosphere for multicultural employees is extensive. Their key policies include mentoring programs, job-shadowing opportunities, career counseling & guidance from top executives, diversity groups, charitable donations to diversity-promoting organizations and inclusion goals that are built-in to managers' performance objectives.

Research has demonstrated that diversity increases the number of different perspectives, styles, knowledge and insights that the team brings to complex problems[3]. The world's most innovative firms, such as *Microsoft*, took advantage of this by introducing multiculturalism in their project teams. Sectors such as manufacturing, IT, aerospace and the construction have taken the lead in such sensitivities. Still, there are other sectors which need knowledge, understanding of intercultural comfort dynamics and support from superiors on managing cross cultural teams in multinational workplaces. Existing models of cross cultures are unable to comprehend the behavior of the employees towards team members coming from different cultural backgrounds. This book fills this important gap in knowledge.

Behavioral aspects among team members require an understanding of all the external and internal factors which influence and motivate team members to behave in certain ways to the cultural comfort of the fellow team members. If these factors are analyzed, it may be possible to separate those factors which are controllable and easily manageable. The effect of the uncontrollable factors may be mitigated by employing other innovative managerial techniques.

Improving team performance

Project performance has been extensively researched by a multiple of researchers[4]. The results of these researches have clearly indicated that the best project performance is achieved when the whole project team is fully aligned with project objectives and is integrated. Within overseas projects, it is essential for organizations to help their project managers to appreciate the international context and develop the abilities to understand the everyday issues from different cultural perspectives.

Typically main focus areas for organizations intending to work overseas are[5]

1. Introduction of practices which balance global competitiveness,
2. Multinational flexibility and
3. The building of global learning capabilities.

This book argues that organizations must develop the cultural sensitivity and abilities to manage and build future capabilities if they are to achieve this balance. However, it should also be noted that linking different individual cultures to project outcomes is controversial. And the understanding of the behavioral process and its real structure in multicultural project teams in most industrial sectors is still in its infancy.

Multiculturalism Vs. cross cultural team effectiveness

While multiculturalism and diversity in work teams can have a positive impact on team performance, if poorly led it can also lead to sub – performance. As suggested in figure 1.1, cross cultural competencies and correct leadership is essential for cross cultural teams.

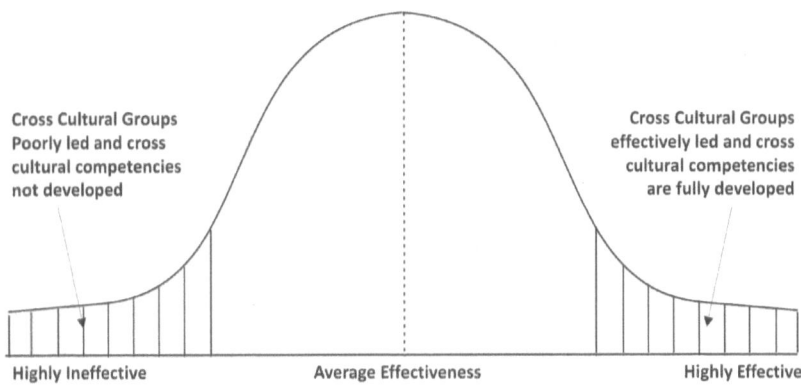

Cross Cultural Groups
Poorly led and cross
cultural competencies
not developed

Cross Cultural Groups
effectively led and cross
cultural competencies
are fully developed

Highly Ineffective   Average Effectiveness   Highly Effective

Figure 1.1: Effectiveness in multicultural teams
(Source: Based on Dr. Carol Kovach's research at Graduate School of Management, UCLA and reported in Nancy J. Adler, International Dimensions of Organizational Behavior, 2nd Edition, PWS – Kent Publishing: 1991)

Highly productive and less productive teams differ in how the diversity is managed and whether so called, cross cultural competencies are developed by the team leaders. Therefore, diversity can be an asset as well as a liability for international project teams depending upon how these are handled in multinational workplaces.

Developing cross cultural competencies

As have been said earlier in the book, efficient management of cross cultural teams can generate useful experience and innovative thinking for international organizations to remain competitive in the marketplace. The framework for such competencies may be based on several research works done is last few decades[6]. According to these researches, such competencies seem to be generally related to the understanding of-

1. Relationships among people from different cultures,
2. Factors affecting motivation of cross cultural team members,
3. Personal lifestyles of members of different cultural background,
4. Differences in terms sensitivity to time, and
5. Socio cultural realities.

In the following paragraphs above aspects of cross cultural understanding by leaders of multinational project teams are described.

Relationships among people from different cultures

For an approach - 'relationship of people among cross cultural teams', two main frameworks of understanding cultural differences have been identified. First, *Hofstede* had identified a cultural dimension called 'individualism versus collectivism' which gives an insight into national cultural differences among nations in terms of the fact that certain national cultures in the world are more individualistic in their behavior than others. Secondly, *Trompenaars* explained this distinction through his own two dimensions – 'individualism versus communitarians' and 'Universalism versus particularism'. These two approaches give important insights into the understanding of how team members with different cultural backgrounds are likely to interact with each other.

However the phenomenon of 'relationship of team members coming from different cultural background' requires a more direct approach than interpreting the above dimensions. This book attempts to study the inquiry into intercultural comfort from a more direct perspective by identifying the underlying observed and latent variables affecting level of comfort, of the members of local cultural groups with members of the foreign cultural group (referred to as 'comfort with foreign cultures (CFC)) within the international work teams at multinational firms. While more literature is available on cross cultural comparison and societal culture's impact on workplaces, the same may not directly deal with the core problem of understanding the 'level of CFC' and quantification of such level of differences among different nations. This book takes cues from the concepts identified by *Hofstede, Trompenaars, House & Javidan* and others along with suggestions related to research on concepts like cultural distance, cultural friction, clashes of cultural identity, cultural diversity, cultural differences, etc. to form a structured theoretical framework which can be used to devise a robust CFC model which can be used to score countries on their 'level of CFC'.

Factors affecting motivation of cross cultural team members

Some of the important factors which may affect the motivation of cross cultural team members would include-

1. Attitude of team managers, especially towards minority groups or alien cultural groups
2. Avenues for equal opportunities,
3. Respecting the opinions of the different cultural groups including

minority groups,

4. Quality of internal communication within the organizations,

5. Level of dedication of the top management towards principle of diversity,

6. Quality of diversity training imparted to employees organization wide and

7. Flexibility of working environment

Multicultural work teams will remain de-motivated if the organizations view diversity in work places as a problem rather than a valuable resource and a possible key success factor. At the same time if certain cultural groups, especially minority groups find that they are deprived of equal career opportunities, unbalanced career growth vis-a-vis their peer groups, and an inflexible working environment, they are bound to be de-motivated and team performance will go down.

Personal lifestyles of members of different cultural background

Personal lifestyles vary significantly among persons from different cultural backgrounds or origins. Some of these differences may be more visible in terms of:

1. Dressing styles.

2. Level of politeness

3. Values and beliefs

4. Body language (like - eye contact, expression of affection, greeting styles)

5. Religious beliefs

6. Personal etiquettes (including dining etiquette, board room etiquette etc.)

7. Spoken language and accent

If understood properly, these differences are not likely to pose any serious challenge to team performance. Rather, organizations must promote a culture of appreciation of these differences. It will make the working environment more conducive to better performance and an emergent & robust organizational culture. Many of these differences can be understood through *Hofstede's* topology of five 'national cultural dimensions'.

Differences in terms of sensitivity to time

An originating culture's definition of time may influence the different working styles of team members originating from different cultures.

Misunderstanding may occur in the interpersonal relations of team members as well as team leaders, usually caused by different understanding of 'time' in different cultures. *North Americans* are usually referred to as slaves of time. On the other hand, persons coming from *Latin America* and *Asia* do not share the same attitude. They come from cultures with a slower pace of life (usually associated with warmer climate countries). People from these countries usually do not so much focus on time. Even if they do, they do it for a short period of time. They tend to believe the focus of work in hand is the work itself, regardless of the time it requires or deadlines associated with projects.

Through research, it is believed that due to cultural factors related to sensitivity of time, perception of time can be divided into three categories:

1. Linear separable time
2. Circular traditional time
3. Procedural traditional time

In the first category above, time is perceived as a straight line consisting of past, present and future. Therefore time is perceived as valuable and hence the time spent in past contributes to the future. Most *Europeans* and *North Americans* fall in this category of time sensitivity. In the second category, time is circular and it is believed that the future can't be changed. In other words future is the replay of the past. Therefore time and planning is not so important. In the last category, time spent on an activity as well at the process in important. Time and money are two separable things and the results are determined by efforts instead of time. The sensitivity to time may change over time, among persons in a new environment, although it may take some time.

Team leaders can manage the outcome by having an understanding of differences of the time sensitivity and allocate work according to these differences among team members, so that the team outcome may be in alignment with the project deadlines and quality standards.

Socio cultural realities

Contemporary socio cultural theorists claim that it is through the process of communication that our cultural realities are produced, maintained, repaired and transformed. They further claim that reality is not an objective set of arrangement outside of us, but is constructed through a process of interaction in groups, communities and culture. These realities are carried forward in team members coming from different cultural backgrounds and these can't be ignored by team leaders. (*See exhibit 1.2.*)

Therefore a deeper understanding of these realities associated with different cultures is essential for team leaders and managers to effectively carry out cross cultural management. Organizations need to work in the direction of providing such competencies and skills among their employees to eventually benefit from diversity and multicultural environment.

Exhibit 1.2

Joint Venture of IBM, Toshiba and Siemens

Three top multinationals – *IBM, Toshiba and Siemens* coming from 3 different countries, decided to develop a chip through a joint venture. In their first review meeting, *Siemens* representative were shocked to notice that *Japanese* representative were closing their eyes, seeming to look like as they are sleeping during the meeting (a common practice of overworked *Japanese* executives especially when a part of the meeting agenda does not concern them). The *Japanese* accustomed to work in bigger groups, find it very painful to work in small, independent offices and talk in small groups and speak English.

IBMers complained that *Germans* plan too much. They also opined that *Japanese* avoid clear decisions while reviewing ideas constantly during meetings. These situations created lack of trust among representatives of three companies and an impression circulated in the group that some of the members of the group, are trying to suppress and hold information from the group.

Failure to address these cultural differences and also failure to agree on a common task and process strategies in a multicultural environment can sabotage any such joint efforts. *S. Canney Davison* describes this situation as 'rush to structure' which is very common place especially in newly formed multicultural teams. Participants who fail to understand this situation jumps straight into nuts and bolts of the task, without devoting enough time to consider the interactive process through which task can be effectively achieved, what are the patterns and styles of communication needed, how meetings are to be conducted, how

---

relationships are built and finally how decisions are to be made. In ignoring these issues in the beginning, teams are storing problems for later.

(Source: Snow, C.C., Canney Davison, S., Hambrick, D.C. and Snell, S.A. (1993) Transnational Teams – A Learning Resource Guide, ICEDR Report, 30.)

Understanding and improving intercultural comfort

It has also been ascertained that intercultural comfort among members of multicultural teams stimulates the formation of an emergent team culture. Unlike homogenous or monoculture teams, multicultural teams cannot be based on a pre-existing identity. It is because of the short 'individual project-based life cycle'. It develops and depends on a team culture of straightforward rules, performance expectations and individual perceptions. It was further confirmed that an effective multicultural team has a strong emergent culture as shared individual prospects facilitate communication and team performance. This suggests that the positive effects and trust generated by the perceived shared understanding can fuel performance improvement and boost team effectiveness. Most importantly, effective interaction among project team members can facilitate the formation of a strong emergent team culture.

Multicultural teams are, however particularly susceptible to communication problems that can deform team cohesion. It is so because individuals in multicultural project teams have different perceptions of the environment, motives and behavioral intentions. It was argued that the effects of such differences could be visible in lower team performance due to impeded social cohesion [7]. Further research on team cohesion and team performance showed a positive correlation between these two variables [8]. Another research asserted that cohesive teams respond faster to changes and challenges and are more efficient [9].

Managing cultural differences and cross-cultural conflicts is generally one of the most common challenges to multicultural teams. It is important to know there has been limited research on people's issues in most industrial sectors involving multicultural teams. People management has become more important in international human resource management. This calls for building cohesive teams through a deeper understanding of observed and latent individual behavior of team members related to the comfort of local cultures with foreign cultures.

Comfort with foreign cultures (CFC): A cultural dimension

Cultural dimensions as suggested by contemporary social scientists, have explained cross cultural comparison of certain cultural traits which could effectively profile those cultures and therefore make team managers sensitive to such differences and may be useful in the process of people management. However, such understanding needs to be complimented by a deeper understanding of the psychological and individual factors, which can explain the dynamics of interaction among diverse cultures, particularly from the perspective of the comfort level between the local cultures and foreign cultures (CFC).

Hofstede too offered his judgment on how host societies react to the arrival of foreigners. According to him, the reaction consists of three steps.

- Step (1) locals are curious about how different foreigners are (i.e., the 'zoo' effect).
- Step (2) ethnocentrism occurs, leading to the locals perceiving their cultures as superior to those of the foreigners. And
- Step (3) which takes longer than others to be reached – and which, in fact, may never be reached in some societies – is polycentrism, where locals evaluate the foreigner as having different standards because they are different.

However, this explanation may not provide the comprehensive understanding of the concepts to team managers. The proposed new cultural dimension, i.e. 'level of CFC' describing level of comfort, of local cultures with foreigners in multicultural workplaces in multinational firms, makes such understanding much simpler, by quantifying the level of CFC on a scale of 0 to 100. A higher CFC score thus indicates a higher level of comfort, of local cultures with foreign cultures. This is the main focus area of discussions in this book.

Therefore the issues at hand are to understand-

1. What are the components of 'intercultural group comfort', in cross cultural teams in multinational firms which explain the

phenomenon?

2. What are the visible and invisible cultural elements or variables, which play an important role in such group comfort interplay?
3. How do these hidden cultural elements or variables or scales (CFC scales) behave in psychological and cultural terms?
4. Does the level of CFC vary from country to country (inter country differences)?
5. Does the level of comfort with culturally different persons vary among diverse cultures within project teams of national organizations within a particular nation (intra country differences)?
6. Are there additional control variables other than 'country' and 'city' which may have an important influence on 'level of CFC'?

Cross cultural leadership and CFC

Certain industrial sectors are faced with the daunting task of spending a major time of its project managers in handling team behavior and communications issues. In these sectors such issues assume prime importance to the success and failure of international projects. For example, one sector where this need has been felt with urgency, is the construction sector. While many researchers have investigated culture in the construction industry, understanding of cross cultural communication on multicultural project teams in this sector is not sufficiently developed. There is mounting evidence and opinion that indicate that integrated teamwork is a primary key in efforts towards improving product delivery within the construction industry.

The focus of this book is also to understand the relationship between effective cross cultural leadership (based on cross cultural competencies) and perceived comfort of both major and minor cultural groups of international project teams. The importance of effective cross cultural leadership has been further emphasized in several past researches. It is found that global project management can succeed through effective leadership, cross – cultural communication, and mutual respect [10]. To achieve project goals and avoid cultural misunderstanding, it is necessary that project managers must be culturally sensitive and promote 'creativity and motivation' through flexible leadership.

Cultural patterns at the workplace in a multinational organization reflect wider societal cultural realities. Project managers themselves share the cultures of their own societies and their organizations with their team members. Here the 'level of CFC' becomes an important area to investigate.

The level of CFC as part of the overall group dynamics of cross cultural teams working on international projects is central to effective cross cultural leadership skills, and these dynamics defines the level of overall success of such teams, whose members should be working smoothly and comfortably with their leaders irrespective of their cultural profiles.

Suggested check list of effective management and leadership.

Based on the theory and practice of modern cross cultural management a generally accepted, check list of effective cross cultural management of workforce in global firms is given below. While the checklist is only a suggested path and not a standard scheme suitable for all sectors, it nevertheless serves as a good starting point for creating a cross cultural competency in an organization.

Bottoms up approach: While a commitment to the idea of an open and receptive workforce must originate at the top management, a bottoms-up approach is what is essential for policy making for an effective cross cultural management in a multicultural environment.

Building effective communication: Policies explicitly forbidding prejudiced, stereotyped and discriminating behavior should be consciously included in employee manuals, recruitment checklists, mission/vision statements and other written policy documents. These documents should be easily accessible to all employees. Diversity messages are required to be broadcast in an effective manner to create trust, empathy and common language among team leaders and team members.

Diversity Training: Training programs aimed at fostering awareness of the significance of diversity and multiculturalism in improving the team performance are essential in modern day global business environment. The training program predominantly should focus on two prime areas – awareness and skill building.

Awareness focused programs should be able to share the diversity information of the organization like demographic data, what diversity brings to the company and interactive exercises prompting participants to think about relevant issues and wider view towards different national cultures as well as facilitate self awareness. Skill building exercises should provide specific information about norms and ways of alien cultures and how these may affect communication and behavior.

Looking at individual differences in the context of cultural differences: Individual differences like personality, aptitude and competence must be viewed in the context of cultural differences to gather a larger picture while making perception about individual performance. Managers should be trained not to make quick and biased generalizations about their subordinates and about their behavior.

Listening to all cultural groups: Listening to each individual cultural groups from their perspective, fosters sense of belonging to each employee. It is a means to confirm that company values them irrespective of their origins and cultural background. Ignoring minority cultural groups have been found to have long term problems for global firms.

Aligning reward system: Reward system should be aligned to diversity and should promote it. Adequate opportunities should be given to minority cultural groups for career development and matching growth.

Flexible working environment: Flexible working environment can solve several cultural differences related problems at work places.

Flexibility provides necessary cushion to each cultural group to adjust their norms and likings to working environment and helps motivate all cultural groups to find common working grounds to achieve company goals and objectives.

Sensitivity to values and opinions: Company needs to encourage sensitivities to values and opinions of persons belonging to different cultural backgrounds. Somewhere in these differences of opinion and values are hidden the solutions to the difficult professional problems companies face while operating globally. Hard to find individual ideas emerge from varying values, opinions and experiences.

Consistent follow up on maintaining diversity: It is to be understood that diversity should be maintained as the core company philosophy as well as a core strategy to compete in the market. For this, constant effort must be encouraged by team leaders while selecting and dealing with team members.

Sorting out language issues: Language issues can create an unequal playing field in a multicultural environment. Choice of language in important meetings can create 'winners and losers', as a language is often associated with influence and power. Such situations are particularly sensitive in 'Parent – Subsidiary' communications. For example, take the case of *the English language* which has become the *lingua Franca* of modern business. Therefore *Anglophones* may tend to dominate group discussions ignoring the differences of ability of speaking *English* among certain team members from other linguistic background. Efforts should be made to lessen emotions by insisting that the language chosen to discuss important matters does not belong to a particular clique, but represent the best solution, based on the composition and choice of team members and their level of fluency. Care must be taken to establish a process which addresses this imbalance related to language choice. (See exhibit 1.3 below about a *French – American* joint venture.)

Exhibit 1.3

Language Issues in a French - American Joint Venture

Poul Orleman, manager of a global training and development team of *French-American* joint venture in pharmaceuticals, offer his own experience with solutions to language issues in his firm.

"We make several rules for participants: Speak slowly; ask for clarification at any point; and if someone gets too frustrated in trying to make point in *English*, the participants can revert to their own native language and someone will help and translate. Though rarely used, this 'native language safety valve' has proved very useful on several occasions.

Even if there is no one to translate, the 'switch to revert to native language' releases unnecessary pressure and frustration; and other participants often learn something about the individual's 'true personality'. There is often an amazing transformation in body language, tone of voice, facial expression and confidence when someone switches to his/her native language."

Conclusion

In this chapter, we learnt the theories which form the basic foundation of some of the most common practices of cross cultural management in global firms. It is also understood from this chapter that multiculturalism in project teams can prove to be an asset if led efficiently and managed well. If not it may also result in sub-performance.

There are certain cross cultural competencies which can be learnt by managers and leaders in order to ensure they provide correct leadership and management in a multicultural environment. It is also confirmed that multiculturalism in today's globalized world is not a challenge rather an important element of corporate strategy capable of deriving a competitive advantage. Therefore, cross cultural skills and foreign language competencies have become important elements of effective strategic management in modern global firms.

Definitions

Some of the following definitions will help in better understanding the context of this book and make the communications of the concepts more clear.

Intercultural comfort: Main focus of this book is on the comfort among members of different cultural groups in workplaces of multinational firms, more specifically those working in multicultural international teams. As a start, 'comfort' herein refers to the relative ease and positive understanding in day to day interactions among team members belonging to different cultural groups. This comfort may be the result of certain inherent factors associated with the rooted cultural profiles of such members. These factors could be – different value systems, religious beliefs (associated with specific cultural background), views about their own cultural identity, distinct views about the process and benefits of globalization, culture specific traits with respect to their inherent ease to work with distant cultures (including communication ease, e.g. due to common language) and other similar factors as suggested by social scientists like *Hofstede*, *Trompenaars* and others.

Foreign cultures or cultural groups: In this book, members of multicultural teams have been classified into broadly two categories – Those belonging to local cultural groups (which are most likely to be dominant groups in the team) and those belonging to groups with diverse foreign (distant or foreign) cultural backgrounds. While it is true that many of the team members who may come from foreign origins might be working for a long time in a particular local cultural environment and must have somewhat adapted to local cultural ways of working, it is reasonable to assume that such members still display distinct cultural traits and behavior which clearly differentiate them from the members of local and dominant cultural groups. And such differences in behavior surely have the overtones of their cultural past. Therefore, in this book foreign cultural groups refer to this second category in international teams at multinational firms.

Multinational Firms: Firms around the world can be in different stages of globalization. For example, some of the firms may be just exporting their standardized or slightly modified products to other countries, others may be involved with international markets in deeper ways. Some of the other firms may be having their own subsidiaries, joint ventures, or collaborations in different countries with region specific manufacturing and marketing infrastructure in several countries. There would be yet other firms which may be treating the globe as their major single global market with substantial revenues coming from outside their home countries. The book refers primarily to such multinational firms (MNEs) which are reasonably global in their businesses and employ multicultural work teams to carry out different international projects.

Suggested questions of discussion

1. What are the basic tenets of a typically high performing team? Discuss with examples.
2. Discuss the importance of maintaining the diversity and multiculturalism in modern workplaces of global firms with examples.
3. Discuss advantages and disadvantages of monoculture and multi-cultural teams. Give examples.
4. What are the language related issues which can damage the team performance in a multicultural environment? Discuss with examples.
5. What are the basic steps of effective management of multicultural teams? Discuss with examples.
6. Define the concept of intercultural comfort among team members of a multicultural team.
7. What is the significance of having a deeper understanding of 'level of comfort' between local cultural groups and foreign cultural groups in a multicultural team? Discuss with examples.
8. What are the common challenges faced by multicultural teams to deliver desirable outcomes in global firms? Discuss.
9. What are the ways of building trust among multicultural members of global teams? Discuss with examples.
10. What are the cross cultural competencies which modern managers must possess in order to derive the best performance of multicultural international project teams in global firms?
11. What are the common factors which may affect the motivation of multicultural team members?
12. What is meaning of the term 'socio-cultural realities' of the multicultural team members?

13. Why these realties need to be understood deeply in order to maximize the team performance? Discuss with examples.
14. Why, sometimes linking different individual cultures to project outcomes can be controversial? Discuss with examples.

Notes:

1. Schmalzer, T. & Singh, Rahul (2010). *The effect of study programme on the approaches to learning and studying.* In M. Neubauer, N.S Anuradha, S. Keuchel, eds. *Cross-Cultural Approaches to Learning and Studying— A Comparative Study of Austria, Germany and India,* 2010, Macmillan Publishers India Ltd. Earley, P.C.,

2. Mosakowski, E. (2000). Creating hybrid team cultures: an empirical test of transnational team functioning. *Academy of Management Journal* 43 (1), 26–49.

3. Jehn, K.A., Northcraft, G.B. & Neale, M.A., (1999). Why differences make a divergence: A field study of diversity, conflict and performance in workgroups. *Administrative Science Quarterly* 44, 741–763.

4. Baiden, B.K., (2006). *Framework of the Integration of the Project Delivery Team.* Unpublished Ph.D. Thesis, Loughborough University.

   Chervier, S. (2003). Cross-cultural management in multinational project groups. *Journal of World Business.* 38, 141–149.

   Ochieng, E.G. (2008). *Framework for Managing Multicultural Project Teams.* Unpublished Ph.D. Thesis. Loughborough University.

   Pearson, J.C., Nelson, P.E. (2003). *Human Communication.* McGraw-Hill, New York.

5. Bartlett, C.A. & Goshal, S. (1989). *Managing Across Borders.* Harvard Business School Press, Boston, MA.

6. Aycan, Z., Kanungo, R.N., Mendonca, M., Yu, K., Deller, J., Stahl, G. & Khurshid, A. (2000). "Impact of Culture on Human Resource Management Practices: A Ten Country Comparison", *Applied Psychology – An International Review,* 49(1), 192-220

   Apfelthaler, G. & Domicone, H. (2008). Drawing Wrong Borderlines: The Concept of culture in a pluralist management world, *Problems and Perspectives in Management,* Vol. 6, Issue 2

   Hofstede, G. (1980). *Culture's consequences: International differences in work-related values.* Beverly Hills, CA: Sage.

   Hofstede, G. (1983). The Cultural Relativity of Organizational Practices and Theories, *Journal of International Business Studies,* 14, 1983

   Hofstede, G. (1984). *Culture's consequences: International differences in work-related values.* Newbury Park, CA: Sage

   Hofstede, Geert (1987). "The Applicability of McGregor's Theories in South

East Asia," *Journal of Management Development*, Vol. 6, No. 3, 9-18.

Hoststede, G. (1991). *Culture and organizations: Software of the mind.* London: McGraw-Hill.

Hofstede, G. (1992). *Cultures and organizations: Software of the mind.* New York McGraw-Hill.

Hofstede, G. (1997). *Cultures and Organizations: Software of the Mind.* New York: McGraw Hill.

Hofstede, G. (2001). *Culture's consequences: Comparing values, behaviors, institutions, and organizations across nations.* Thousand Oaks, CA: Sage.

Hofstede, G. (2006). What did GLOBE really measure? Researchers' minds versus respondents' minds, *Journal of International Business Studies*, 37, 882-896.

House, R., Javidan, M. & Dorfman, P. W. (2001). Project GLOBE: An introduction. *Applied Psychology: An International Review*, 50(4), 489-505.

House, R.J. & Javidan, M. (2004). *Overview of GLOBE.* In R. J. House, P.J. Hanges, M. Javidan, P. W. Dorfman, V. Gupta (Eds.), *Culture, leadership and organizations. The GLOBE study of 62 societies* (pp. 9-28). Thousand Oaks, CA: Sage Publications.

House, R.J., Javidan, M., Dorfman, P.W. & de Luque, M.S. (2006). A failure of scholarship: Response to George Graen's critique of GLOBE. *Academy of Management Perspectives*, 102-114.

Trompenaars F. & Hampden-Turner, C. (1997). *Riding the waves of culture: Understanding diversity in global business (2nd Ed.).* New York: McGraw-Hill.

7. Shaw, M.E. (1981). *Group Dynamics: The Psychology of Small Group Behavior.* McGraw-Hill, New York.

8. Evans, C.E., Dion, K.L. (1991). Group Cohesion and Performance. *Small Group Research* 22, 175–186.

9. Elron, E. (1997). Top management teams within multinational corporations: Effects of cultural heterogeneity. *The Leadership Quarterly* 8 (4), 355–393.

10. Anbari, F.T., Khilkhanova, E.V., Romanova, M.V. & Umpleby, S.A. (2004). *Journal of International Business and Economics*, Vol II, No.1

Online resources for this chapter, available at:
http://www.vijeshjain.com/books/multinational-workplaces/resources/chapter-1

2. UNDERSTADNING CULTURES

This chapter moves from defining the culture to the historical use of the term culture, as understood in anthropology, humanities and in common parlance. It further discusses the concepts of 'gradual cultural change', national cultures and organization cultures. It also describes some of the most discussed elements of culture which identify and differentiate national and regional cultures. Also discussed are the researches done to define different cultural dimensions of national cultures by some of the renowned social scientists of modern times. A description of the types of popular cultures is also given. A peculiar issue related to *American* culture is discussed in the exhibit 2.1 below.

Exhibit 2.1

Why are *Americans* so happy, gregarious and positive?

American culture is characterized by generally being happier, more gregarious and more optimists. The data compiled by *YSC Bains'* consulting firm, shows 35% of American executives display positivity traits, compared to only close to 20% of Chinese or *Indian* executives.

To understand the cultural DNA of *America* one must revisit the history of *America* since 500 years back. The first people to arrive in *America* from *Europe* were *Puritans* followed by *Quakers*, who settled in *Northern* part of *US*. Next ones were a section of *British landed*

---

aristocracy. While these all batches of settlers were quite different from each other in cultural terms. they still had one thing in common. They were all ready to travel 3500 miles across *Atlantic* to preserve their distinctive political and religious beliefs in the face of prosecution in their homeland. *America* was seen by the *Old Europeans* to be the New World. A chance for them to escape from the drudgery of feudal society, malnutrition (particularly in the case of the *Irish* who went to the *US* in droves during the 1840's *potato famine*), the weight of family tradition and a real opportunity for religious tolerance. Typically those who came from other parts of the globe after the first wave of *European* migration came for similar reasons - with the exception of blacks who were brought as slaves and *Chinese* who were brought as cheap labor for building the railroads. One can't be sure if this has affected these particular ethnic groups concept of happiness within their lives in the *US*. But generally most people chose to come to the *US* and they did so with hope and optimism to build themselves a better life. This powerful thinking prevails even today.

From a political perspective when the founding fathers of the *US* wrote the constitution they did think to include the right to happiness - which is something that is believed to be almost unique in terms of written constitutions. But knowing that they have the right to be happy must surely have a subconscious impact on their day to day living and it should feel natural, rather than something which is sinister, forced or derided as it sometimes is in many of the other cultures on this planet.

Local dominant cultures in project teams have been found to behave in a manner which has, sometimes caused cross cultural teams to perform lower[1]. Cultural issues among team individuals can cause conflict, misunderstanding and poor performance[2]. The understanding of the behavioral dynamics of multicultural project teams in certain industrial sectors is still in its infancy[3]. It was also found that the lagging industrial sectors in this area need to address their poor performance in terms of people management in international project teams, by focusing on their cultural issues[4].

This book proposes that such behavior generally emanates from lower 'comfort of local cultures with foreign cultures (CFC)', which is central to the cross cultural issues facing managers of international project teams in multinational firms. This level of CFC needs further investigation and understanding to enable project managers to deal with the jerks and glitches caused by observed and unobserved behavior of members of cross cultural teams in multinational firms, thereby ensuring improved results from more integrated and aligned teams.

Five of the most distinctive challenges international project managers in multinational firms, face are:

1. Managing cultural diversity, differences and conflicts,
2. Developing team cohesiveness;
3. Maintaining communication richness;
4. Dealing with coordination and control issues and
5. Handling geographic distances and dispersion of teams [5].

At the core of the issues of facing these challenges are the ones that relate to the understanding of intercultural comfort dynamics. In the following paragraphs terms 'culture' and 'cultural differences' have been discussed in some details for a deeper understanding of the main subject of this book.

Historical use of the term 'Culture'

The concept of culture first seems to appear from the term used in classical antiquity by *Roman* orator *Cicero*, as *'cultura anime'* which means cultivation of the soul. The concept reemerged in modern *Europe* in the 17th century, referring to 'refinement of people' through education.

In 18th and 19th century the concept of culture frequently referred in discussions about 'national aspirations and ideals'. In the 20th century, term 'culture' reemerged as the central theme of 'anthropology', usually referring to a range of human phenomenon that cannot be attributed to genetic inheritance. For example *Hoebel* described culture to be an integrated system of patterns of learned behavior which are characteristics of the members of a society and which are not a consequence of biological inheritance. Culture is a central aspect of anthropology, referring to a range of phenomenon, described through social learning and human societies. The word seems to represent the evolved ability of humans to categorize and express human experiences through symbols or expressions.

These representations are refined over the time through the ability of humans to act more imaginatively and creatively to express more and more clearly to each other. Anthropologists report such behavioral modernity evolved among humans in last 50000 years and seems to be unique to humans when compared with other living creatures on our planet. Other living creatures have also demonstrated evolution of such ability but in much less complex forms. Anthropologists believe, evolution of such capabilities of humans have resulted into more complex behavior of humans in the forms of languages; social practices like - kinship, gender and marriages; expressive forms such as rituals, dance, music, religion; technologies like – cooking, housing, clothing, personal upkeep and beautification; material aspects of culture such as – architecture, art, technologies; and immaterial aspects like – philosophy, political organization, social institutions, mythology, literature and science.

The meaning of word 'culture' as understood in 'social sciences' broadly refers to a complex whole which may include – knowledge, art, beliefs, morals, law, customs, and any of the capabilities or habits acquired by man as a member of a society [6]. In common parlance, 'culture' is a set of customs, traditions, values and heritage of a society or community such as an ethnic group or nation. Sometimes it also refers to specific practices within sub groups and often identified as 'sub culture' within cultures.

In cultural anthropology, it is often claimed that cultures cannot be objectively evaluated or ranked since any such comparison, ranking, or evaluation is situated within a given value system of the culture represented by the evaluator himself. Therefore, it appears that concept of low and high culture is misnomer even if contested by the fact of stratified access of different cultural groups in the 'cultural capital'. In this sense 'multiculturalism' seems to be referring to a political ideology that values the 'useful' and 'peaceful' coexistence and mutual respect among different cultures sharing and living in the same geographical territory, region, organization or nation.

Another definition of culture is, 'the bearer of human wisdom and includes a wealth of human behaviors, beliefs, attitudes, values and experiences of immense worth' [7]. Culture is also defined as, 'an integrated pattern of human behavior, including thoughts, communication, ways of interacting, roles and relationships, and expected behaviors, beliefs, values, practices and customs' [8]. According to another perspective, culture refers to 'the values, norms and traditions that affect how individuals of a particular group perceive, think, behave and make judgments about the world around them' [9]. In addition, the concept of 'culture' also carries attributes which are most 'dear' or which are most 'offensive' to a member of a culture. These attributes too could be different for different cultures across the world.

The modern meaning of culture is popularly based on a term first used in classical antiquity using agricultural metaphor, for the development of a philosophical soul [10]. *Samuel Pufendorf* took over this metaphor by refereeing to culture as 'all ways in which human beings overcome their original barbarism, and through artifice, become fully human'. 18th century *German* thinkers in their writings tried to contrast between 'culture' and 'civilization'. These writings give most of the modern meaning to the culture. Two primary meanings emerged from this period – 'culture' as the folk spirit having a unique identity and 'culture' as cultivation of waywardness or free individuality. Interestingly, these meaning no more discussed the cultivation of philosophical soul, the earlier core philosophy surrounding the term 'culture'.

Cultural change

The central theme of modern meaning of 'culture' is 'change'. Today humanity is in a global period of ever accelerating 'cultural change', driven by the expansion and democratization of technology, information, finance, population growth, international commerce, a dynamic geopolitical environment throughout the globe and other factors. Cultural changes are internally the result of interaction of two counter forces – one that is forcing change and the other which is resisting change. These two forces are related to both social structures and 'events & happenings'. These are acted upon by perpetuation of newer cultural ideas and practices within current structures which themselves are subject to change [11]. Some of the drivers of cultural change are discussed below:

1. The advancement of technologies and social conflicts can produce cultural changes by altering social dynamics and introduction of new cultural models, forcing ideological and other changes. For example, successful feminist movement in *the US*, forced shift in gender relations, altering both gender and economic structures.

2. 'Natural and environmental' events can force cultural changes. For example, return of tropical forests after the end of the ice age, led to the domestication of certain plants and the invention of agriculture, resulting in major changes in 'social and economic structures' throughout the world, changes accelerated by several new 'cultural innovations' [12].

3. Diffusion and acculturation among different societies can also affect cultures externally, which can produce or inhibit social shifts,

changes in cultural practices and transfer of cultural ideas.

4. War and competition over limited resources can have an impact on social dynamics and technological development.

At the same time there can be various other factors which can drive cultural change. In order to understand the impact and process of cultural change, it is important to understand the most important cultural elements which form the very basis of a societal culture and distinguish one culture from another. These cultural elements are discussed in following paragraphs.

Elements of culture

Culture combines many elements to shape the way a group of people live together. Depending upon the size of the group, these elements can be identified in many ways. If culture refers to a smaller set of people say a small & remote village, it can be identified through a few of these elements and can be differentiated from another culture of another similar group using these or similar elements. However, if the culture refers to a larger set of people say, national culture referring to a culture of the whole nation, identification of cultural element will take a different approach. In national cultural comparison, it may be difficult to compare nations based on a simple set of cultural elements. Nevertheless, there are certain most common cultural elements which differentiate national cultures. Since the theme of this book is more concerned with the national cultures, it identified mainly following seven major elements which even if not exhaustive, may shape a national culture.

Social Organization

Social organization denotes the way a society is divided into smaller units to meet its basic needs. The most common of such smaller units include family patterns and social classes. Family patterns may differ in different cultures in being joint family structure, nuclear family structure, extended family structure or other forms of family structures. A typical family structure of an industrialized country is characterized by a father, mother and children. However, different family structures may characterize different countries depicting unique characteristics of different national cultures.

Relationships, communication and behavior of family members may also vary from one culture to another. For example, some of the cultures are characterized by a higher level of respect of elders by the younger ones.

Similarly, social classes rank members of the society, in order of their importance to the group depending upon what may be more important to that culture. Depending upon the importance given to a particular aspect like – money, job, education, and ancestry, importance are attached to different members of the society. The decisions and rituals of the society are mostly acceptable to the other members of the society. Such rankings can also characterize one culture as different from another.

Customs and Traditions

Customs and traditions are enforced ideas of perceived 'right' and 'wrong' which may be unique to a particular culture. These ideas give birth to different customs, traditions, rules and / or written laws which are enforced in a society and all members are expected to adhere to these ideas or face opposition from a majority of the members of the group. These customs and traditions may even relate to things like - what to eat; how to dress; whom to marry; whom not to marry; what kind of education one must have and so on. Even functional roles may be defined in a society based on birth in a family with a specific status given by the society's customs and traditions.

Religion

Religion refers to a way of life adopted by a society based on a set of answers to the basic meaning and purpose of life. Members of a particular religion may be expected to live their life in a particular way as described by his or her religion. Religious leaders are entrusted with job of guiding religious members to embrace a particular way of life and answer their doubts related to 'creation' and 'creator' on one hand and 'material' and 'non material' things of life on the other. Spiritual discourse plays an important role in defining the meaning of life and life style prescribed in a particular religion.

Different cultures may display varying levels of adherence of religious behavior by the members of the group. Most of the religions focus more on non materialistic life. Most industrialized societies are typically characterized by their more materialistic ways of living, while many of the developing and under developed cultures stand by non materialistic ways of life. Importance given to specific religion also varies from one culture to another.

Most religious cultures believe their way of life being better than others and perceive it as their duty to propagate their religious ideas to cover more and more groups of societies and expand the reach of their religion. Such ambitions and sense of duties have also created major global conflicts, even wars and also believed to have given birth to a sense of superiority over others among certain cultural groups. More recently, terrorism is also found to have religious overtones and the basis.

Language

Language is the cornerstone of different cultures. Language makes it more comfortable for members of a society to communicate and better understand each other. However, differences of language over geographical distances also create communication barriers among different cultures and sometimes may even lead to misunderstanding, biases and stereotypes. Therefore language also serves as a major identifier of different cultural groups or even national cultures. Origins of different languages and dialects among different cultural groups also indicate long isolation of different cultural groups in human history, resulting in different levels of cultural development and lack of awareness of the other's ways of life that exists in different cultures. People who speak same or similar languages often have been found to share similar ways of life and culture.

There are about 122 major languages and 1599 other languages which are spoken in different regions and provinces of India. Most of these languages are understood by the local communities only and outsiders find it extremely difficult to understand the local languages. No wonder India is home to communities with significantly different cultures, lifestyles and perception about life.

Arts and Literature

Arts and literature are the products of human imagination, creativity and a strong sense of depicting best of a particular culture to its own members as well as to the members of the other cultures or even to the future generations of different cultures. These also serve as the record of beliefs and way of life of a particular culture during a particular time. Some of the arts and literature are also the product of one's choice of profession and urge to show one's talent to the other members of a society. Arts and literature helps pass one culture's beliefs and ideas to future generations. These can be in the different forms of arts, music, folk dances and folk tales.

Forms of Government

People form governments to bring order in their life based on their culture and their way of life. The governments help the society to meet its basic needs, preserve its culture and help the members of the society from the onslaught of outside forces such as physical attacks, economic upheavals, religious propaganda and other cultural threats. Differences in the forms of government formed by different national groups indicate specific needs of the national cultures and form an important element of those cultures.

Gastronomy

Gastronomy etymologically refers to 'the art or law of regulating the stomach'. It is an all encompassing term, subsuming all of cooking techniques, nutritional facts, science of food and all that relates to palatability, taste and smell related to human ingestion. Gastronomy therefore refers to all about discovering, tasting, experiencing, researching, understanding and writing about cuisines, food preparations as well about nutrition interfaces with broader cultures. Gastronomical studies tell a lot about a particular culture. On a global scale gastronomy significantly differentiates national and regional cultures. Most cultures are extremely loyal to their own recipes, way of cooking of their own kinds of food and feel proud of their own gastronomical identity. These cultures, like their religious beliefs, tend to propagate their gastronomical ways of life to other cultures.

Entertainment

Entertainment is a set of activities which hold the attention and interest of the people, or gives delight and pleasure. While the common medium of entertainment is – storytelling, theater, music, dance, different types of performances, the preferences of people vary and may be unique to specific cultures developed over thousands of years in different cultural groups. In modern times the process of entertainment has been highly influenced by technology, resulting into multibillion dollar entertainment industries around the people of the world. Despite its global reach, regional preferences still prevail and different cultures strongly identify themselves with their own ways of entertainment.

Sports

Sports is a set of physical and competitive activities which helps people to engage themselves in certain periods of times and also provides entertainment, skills and mental abilities. It holds people's attention and is very useful for maintaining communal harmony and calm among members of the society. It can also be a cross cultural and competitive physical activity. Preferences of the nature and forms of sports activities vary among different cultures, preferences have developed over thousands of years. (*See exhibit 2.2 below*)

Exhibit 2.2

Why are there *Chinatowns* in almost all major cities in the world?

While there are several historical reasons in different part of the world for *Chinese* to prefer to live with relatively secluded lifestyle in the form of *Chinatowns* in major cities of the world, one important aspects of *Chinese* culture is their being historically an introverted country which held an internal image of its own and sense of superiority over others. Historically rulers of *China* avoided any cultural exchange with the outside world for its people in order to protect their own culture and political setup. Though *Chinese* have developed skills in ship construction and navigation fairly early, the rules were eventually made to ban any manufacturing of large ships and forbade long voyages overseas. The famous seven long voyages of *Admiral Cheng Ho* in the fifteenth century were brought to a halt by the third generation of the all powerful *Ming Dynasty* rulers who deemed such explorations frivolous and destroyed almost all evidences of such voyages so that others does not harbor such exploratory ambitions.

As per a research in *US* universities, *Chinese* students are found to keep to themselves and interact less with other cultures. Similarly in *Africa*, there are large communities of *Chinese* skilled and unskilled persons. But here too they have been observed to remain cut off from local societies, eating their own foods and preferring to employ their own *Chinese* staff to look after the daily chores. *Chinatowns* of *London, San Francisco, Kula Lumpur, Singapore, Sydney,* although are different from each other, but they are all some form of recreation of their home country

---

Semiotics of culture and language

In modern times, certain researchers have tried to study the culture from a semiotic point of view, as a type of human symbolic activity, creation of signs and a way of giving meaning to everything around. In this perspective, culture is understood as a system of symbols or meaningful signs. It is also closely related to linguistics. Researchers of semiotic perspective viewed culture as a hierarchical system of semiotics, consisting of a set of correlated functions, and linguistic codes that are used by social groups to maintain the coherence.

If we call the collection of all sign systems in the world as *'semiosphere'*, then one can say that cultural semiotics is the cultural part of this *'semiosphere'*. Therefore, cultural semiotics offers the theoretical foundations for answering following possible questions.

1. How do the signs and sign systems in different cultures differ from natural signs and sign systems?

2. What determines the boundaries and identity of a culture?

3. How does cultural change originate?

4. How does cultures of the world relate to each other in *'semiosphere'*?

In other words, 'cultural semiotics' provides a more scientific framework for empirical investigation and cross cultural comparison. One example of the use of the concept of semiotics is given in the exhibit 2.3 below referring to colors as a sign system studied with the perspective of semiotics.

Exhibit 2.3

Semiotics of cultures: Colors

Before the collapse of communism in *Eastern Europe*, there was a joke about colors doing rounds in different parts of *America*:

Someone informed *USA* officials that the *Russians* were planning to paint entire moon red to show their supremacy in space. *US* official said. "Ok, no problem, let them paint the moon red." They added "We'll just write *Coca-Cola* on top of it and everybody will know who the best is…"

This is joke but has a powerful meaning of colors in different cultures of the world.

During its 1994 launch campaign, *European* mobile phone company –

Orange – had to change its ads in *Northern Ireland*. "The future's bright, the future's *Orange*." This was offensive in *Northern Ireland* because in the *North* the term *Orange* suggests the 'Orange Order' signifying Protestant, loyalist…

Here are a few things one must k now about colors and their meaning in different cultures:

Red

Red is the color of love in most cultures: *Chinese* brides wear red for their wedding, and red roses are the most common gift for St. Valentine's Day.

In *Christianity*, green and red are associated with *Christmas*. There is an *Easter* tradition to color eggs red – red in this case represents the blood of *Christ*.

Red is also the color of communism – the flags of *China* and *Vietnam* are red. The Former *Soviet Union's* flag used to be red too. The army of the *Soviet Union* was known as the "*Red Army*".

Satan is also most of the time represented by the color red in icons and popular culture. On the other hand, *Santa Claus* wears red and white for *Christmas*.

In *China*, red paper and red envelopes are frequently used to wrap gifts of money. Though, on the negative side, obituaries are traditionally written in red ink, and to write someone's name in red signals that you are either cutting them out of your life, or that they have died.

Red is also used to indicate emergencies and warnings. Red is the color for all Stop signs around the World. However, the first Stop sign had black letters on a white background until 1924 when white was replaced with yellow. It wasn't until 1954 that all stop signs became white and red. World's largest humanitarian organization helping in emergencies is 'International *Red Cross*'.

Green

In *North America*, because of the color of the *United States* dollar bill, green is the color of wealth and money. Also, the color green is always associated with nature. In *Romania*, people with green eyes are seen as very deceptive people. In some of *Shakespeare's* plays, envy is associated with the color green

White

While *Westerns* see white as the color of purity and innocence, in some *Asian* cultures (*China*, *Vietnam*, and *Korea*), white is the color of death and mourning. In *India*, people wear white after the death of a family member. White is the traditional color of bridal dresses in *Western* cultures. A woman wearing white will be seen as a bride on a *Western* website, and as a person in mourning on an *Eastern* website.

White is also the color of snow and winter. Some associate snow with *Christmas*, forgetting that countries from the *Southern hemisphere* don't have snow during *Christmas* time.

A white pigeon is an international sign of peace; a white flag is an international sign of surrender.

Blue

Iran: mourning

China: immortality; workers' uniforms; blue-colored gifts are associated with death

Hinduism: the color of *Krishna*

Egypt: dark blue is a color of mourning.

Black

Black is the color of mourning in *Western* cultures;

Black is also the most common color used for clothing for formal occasions; black is also worn by priests.

In the *Japanese* culture, until the nineteenth century, some women used to dye their teeth black because it was thought that black teeth would make a woman look beautiful.

Orange

The colors orange and black are the colors of *Halloween* because orange is the color of *pumpkins* and black is the color of night and darkness.

Orange is the national color of the *Netherlands*, referring to the royal family, the House of *Orange-Nassau*.

Orange is the brand used by *France Telecom* for its mobile network operator and Internet service provider subsidiaries.

Cultural Groups

According to the anthropological history of humankind, certain human weaknesses and psychological factors - like inability to move fast on the vast planet; desire to explore and know the unknown; desire to look for new resources to make life easier etc. resulted in slowly moving of different persons at different times all over the planet and form distinct groups over time, forgetting their own origins across generations. These cultural groups formed communities, nations, distinct societies, religions, civilizations and political enclaves, characterized by patterns of relationships between individuals who shared distinct cultures and institutions. A given society, for example, may be described as the sum total of such relationships among its members.

Types of Cultures

In many ways, a culture refers to a set of shared values, belief and attitudes. Cultures, therefore, can be categorized in several ways and situations leading to different categories of groups, sharing common beliefs, values and attitudes. Moreover the existence of several elements of culture which defines a culture makes it very difficult to categorize them in a well defined set of typologies. Therefore, when we talk about types of cultures, we tend to categorize in terms of the context of the reference. For example, when we are discussing organizational cultures from a purely business and commercial point of view, we define cultures of a group of persons based on organizational practices. Similarly, when we talk about categorizing society culture in a general way, we tend to stratify cultures from the point of view of common societal practices. We also tend to use different methods of categorization for cultures when we studied from different perspectives, say in rural perspective, or urban perspective or national perspective and so on. In following paragraphs some most useful types of cultures are described and discussed, in several contexts.

Organizational cultures

Organizational culture roughly refers to human behavior at workplaces and the meaning that people and the internal and external stakeholders of the organization attach to those behaviors. An organization may also include its vision, mission, values, norms, systems, symbols, language, assumptions, beliefs and habits. It may also depend on the type of organization, type of work culture, leadership and policies of the organization. There is a large variety of organizational cultures which materialize either naturally or dictated silently (or not so silently) by higher ups. These workplace ethos guides people how they should behave among themselves, with the customer and with the management of the organization.

A typical set of types of organizational cultures commonly observed and discussed is given below

Academy culture – This kind of organizational culture is mostly observed in places like universities, hospitals, research organizations, medical colleges and other types of educational and research institutions. These are commonly represented by highly educated work force that are studious, welcome 'on the job learning' and willing to be trained further in useful skills and knowledge.

Organizations which are characterized by this type of organizational culture are seen to be very careful about - whom they hire; existing and required skill sets and are willing to invest in further learning and training of the work force. Normally these types of organizations have lower employee turnover rates and employees are motivated to do their jobs to the best of their present and future abilities.

Normative cultures – This is the most commonly observed organizational culture which is characterized by comparatively mechanical types of work culture. Employees rarely deviate from the assigned nature and methodology of the job functions. These organizations are run like tight ships and may not be suited for all types of employees. These organizations are mostly run based on certain sticky rules and employees are penalized for breaking these rules. These organizations, mostly follow 'tops – down' approach of leadership.

Pragmatic culture – This type of culture is observed in organizations which are highly customer centric and the only rule is - customer is always right. The customer and clients come first before anything else. Whatever customers want, employees have to work to provide them. Many of the hospitality companies, travel companies, luxury hotels, passenger transportation companies, cruise management companies follow such type of culture.

Club culture – This type of culture is characterized by the 'best in the industry' ethos. Best educational qualification, best past experience, personal interests and demonstrated industry leadership qualities are the norms of each level of employees who work under such cultures. Frequent role changes, multiple yearly appraisals, intense hiring processes are the norms in club culture types of organizations. Strong references are required for each hire. Some of the best examples of club cultures can be seen in organizations like the *FBI*, certain top airlines, top business schools, certain elite military branches, etc. Employees are highly rewarded for their exclusive performances but are always under constant watch of the superiors to perform.

Base Ball Team Cultures – This type of culture is becoming increasing popular among companies where employees with special skills and talent are required. These organizations are employee focused and go extra mile to keep them happy in terms of work environment, compensation, career growth, work-life balance, etc. Some examples of this type of organizational culture are seen in many IT companies like *Google, Microsoft, Intel Corporation, Dell* and *Apple* etc.

Fortress Culture – This type of culture is mostly seen in sales oriented companies. The job security is based purely on performance in such organization. You get paid very well if you can perform otherwise you are bound to exist. Termination rates rather than employee turnover is high in such organizations. This type of culture is more common in companies selling highly competitive products like, FMCG goods, insurance products, financial products etc.

Tough Guy Culture – Many call center agencies, or customer relation companies develop this type of work culture in their organization where employees are constantly monitored for using a set protocol and behavior to deal with the customers. Deviations are recorded and employees are subjected to frequent training if they deviate from the scripted job profiles. Employees are micro – managed in this kind of culture.

Process Culture – Process culture is normally seen in many government run organizations in certain countries. While employees are not micro-managed, rules and regulations are framed, under which each employee is supposed to function. The process is well defined as soon as an employee joins and he knows what he or she has to do with the organization. A type of ideology has to be adhered to by each employee in line with the domain under which the organization functions. Often an employee finds loopholes in the written rules and regulations to get a job done in a particular way. The organization is more process driven than vision driven. Functional autonomy is lacking in such cultures.

Risk Takers – This type of culture is more common in certain organizations in individualistic cultures like *US* and many *Western European* countries where organizations are dependent on success and failure of individual ideas of most influencing employees. Decisions are taken by certain employees betting on the success of the idea without any guarantee on the success. The stakes are normally higher on such decisions. Success is very profitable and failure can doom the companies. One example of such organization is *Apple* where employees are encouraged to take risks in pursuit of success through new and novel ideas.

National Cultures

Cultures vary a lot not only among continents, but also among countries. This brings us to the concept of 'national cultures'. The concept of national cultures has to do with differences between national cultural background of individuals in their business environment. The concept has also to do with the way those manifested differences may influence business decisions at the international level. National culture can be interpreted as "a common frame of reference or logic by which members of a nation view organizations, the environment, and their relations to one another." [13] There are both tangible and intangible expressions of 'behavioral modernity' evolved over a very long time of human history giving birth to unique cultures on different points on earth having gone through different experiences and environments.

Anthropologists also report that such cultural differences are also the results of certain weaknesses of the human race as discussed earlier, resulting into different cultural pockets around the world; competition for limited resources to survive, resulting into formation of geographical groups of humans; differences of external bodily appearances caused by differing climatic conditions of living at different places on earth, resulting into human group formations based on similar external bodily features and other similar criteria.

From the humanities perspective, culture refers to the evolution of individual attributes, the degree to which individuals or individual cultures have cultivated a particular level of sophistication in terms of mannerism, education, arts, music, sciences, justice, habits and philosophy. This level of sophistication also refers to deferring level of complexities of societies and distinguishing one civilization from another. This hierarchical perspective seems to have resulted into emergence of class based cultural differences or cultural groupings, giving credence to the beliefs of the existence of the higher classes of cultures as compared to lower classes, so called high culture or elite cultures when compared with low cultures, folk cultures or popular cultures, represented by lower classes. More recently, the concepts of 'mass cultures' have emerged to refer to so called politically created 'mass produced' or 'mass mediated' forms of 'consumer cultures', that emerged in the last century. It is not uncommon in cultural studies that, culture is used politically as a tool of elites to manipulate the lower classes and create false consciousness, as also claimed in the philosophy of '*Marxism*' and 'critical theory'.

In more recent times, a lot has been discussed in humanities about similar looking consumer cultures, so called 'cosmopolitan world cultures' which are the result of a common set of living conditions in large metro cities of the world, irrespective of their geographical locations, mediated by the use of a common set of mass produced goods and services in these large cities.

National cultures have been categorized differently by different social scientists. Some of the common categories of national cultures which are discussed in cross cultural studies are described in following paragraphs.

High Context cultures - High context cultures are characterized through the tendency to use high context messages, resulting in these cultures catering to in-groups. In routine communication, many things are left unsaid, leaving the culture to explain. A few words can communicate a complex message very effectively to in-groups (less effectively to an out-group). Many *Asian* cultures like *Indian, Chinese* and even *European* cultures like *Hungarian* culture lies in this category of cultures. Such cultures rely heavily on implicit messages and contextual cues.

Low Context Cultures - These cultures do not cater towards in-groups. Low context cultures do not rely on contextual elements like tone, body languages, etc. and uses a direct approach to communicate a message able to cater to both in-groups as well as out-groups. Relationships are for short periods and exist for specific reasons. Following procedures and keeping sight of the goals are important in accomplishing any transaction.

High Group Cultures - High group cultures are defined under a new theory called group – grid theory. According to this theory people are strongly bonded together in groups in high group cultures. They spend more time together and have relatively stable relationships. In management terms high group cultures manage resources better. When people are grouped together strongly, laws are more easily defined and policed. People have connected sense of identity, relating more deeply and personally to one another.

Low Group Cultures - Contrary to high group cultures, in low group cultures, people are less connected to each other. For society to survive when internal bonds are weaker and central control is less, individuals must display the highest level of self restraints. In low group cultures if people fail to display self restraints, societies are bound to fail eventually. In management, low group cultures are found to management resources poorly.

High Grid Cultures - The grid phenomenon in cultures refers to how different people are placed in a group and how they take on different roles. In high grid cultures, there are distinct roles and positions within the group with specialization and different accountability. There are different types of entitlement and privileges depending on the position. There may be differing balance of exchange between and across individuals. In management, high grid cultures are found to manage needs better.

Low Grid Cultures - In low grid cultures, people are relatively homogeneous in their abilities, work and activity; and therefore are suited to changing roles rather easily. This makes them less dependent on each other. Low grid cultures are found to be able to manage needs less efficiently.

Fatalistic cultures - According to the group – grid theory (see figure 2.1), cultures which display, low group phenomenon but higher grid phenomenon display fatalistic attributes. For example less obligation of 'haves' towards 'have-nots'. Individuals are left to their fates, which may be positive or negative for them. People feel isolated from each other and display apathy and avoidance. These cultures are characterized by power imbalance and leaderships are mostly despotic. Such cultures, neither manage resources, nor needs efficiently.

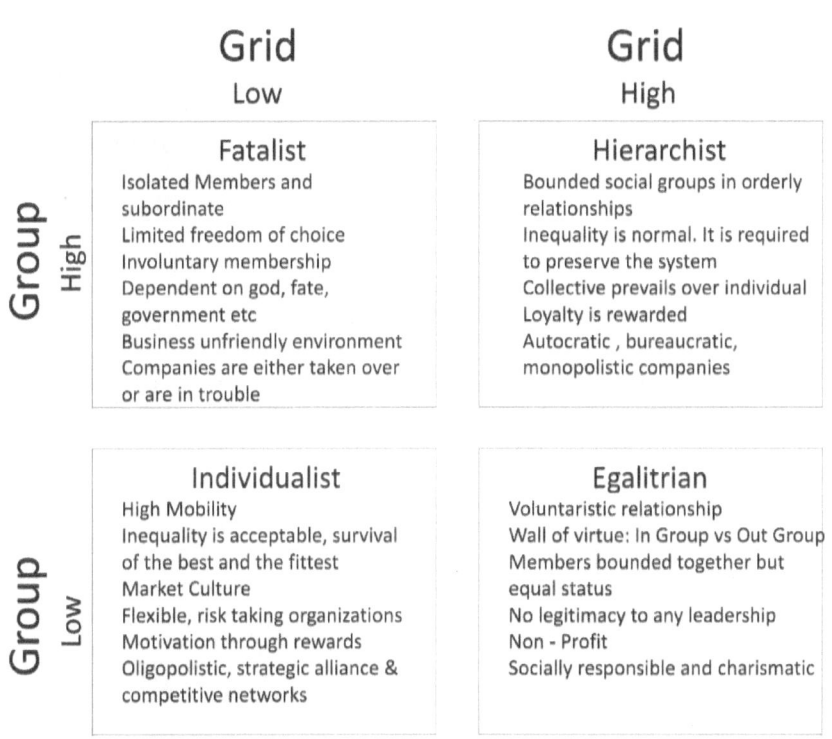

Figure 2.1: Group Grid Cultural Model

Collectivist cultures - Collectivist cultures are those which display high group as well as high grid attributes. These cultures are characterized by developing stronger institutions, hierarchies and laws which regulate individual action and provide for weaker members of the society. The risks are generally managed by national rules. Members of the society are supposed to be obedient to the central power. The society is managed by bureaucrats. Leadership is positional. Such societies are found to manage resources well, but not the needs of the people.

Individualistic cultures - Also known as market cultures, this type of culture is more popular among democratic societies. Characterized by low grid and low group phenomenon, people are relatively similar yet have fewer obligations to each other. People enjoy their differences more than their similarities and seek to avoid central authority. However to survive the key is 'self regulations and self restraints' because if those are missing, such a society tends to become a fatalistic society. Risks are equated with opportunities in such cultures. Such cultures manage both needs and resources efficiently.

Egalitarian cultures – This type represents a high group - low grid, culture, having less central rules than collectivist societies. But for such culture to survive the key requirement is that each member voluntarily helps each other. Therefore, it is not rules than prevail, but the values which are appreciated. People enjoy similarities because this leads to agreement and adoption of similar values. Integrity of individuals is the key for survival of such cultures. Leadership is generally charismatic. Such cultures manage needs well, but not the resources.

Hermit cultures - There are certain cultures which retreats from whatever types of other cultures exist on this planet. They live as hermits, interacting with others only when necessary.

Other classifications of cultures

Cultures have been variously classified in different contexts other than the contexts mentioned above. Some of the commonly discussed cultures in management education are:

Consumer cultures - Consumer culture is characterized by a society based on consumerism. The theory of consumer culture focuses on consumer choices and consumer behavior from a social and cultural point of view rather than from an economic or psychological point of view. It predominantly refers to a family of theoretical perspectives that address the dynamic relationships between consumer actions, the marketplace and cultural meanings. Consumer culture is viewed as a social arrangement in between living culture and social resources. It is also a relation between meaningful ways of life and the symbolic and material resources, on which members of society depend. These relations are mediated through markets and consumers as part of an interconnected system of commercially produced goods and images which they use to construct their identity in their mind and orient their relationship with others.

Coffee Culture - Coffee culture refers to a social atmosphere or a series of associated social behaviors that depend heavily on the commodity called 'coffee', where this commodity works as a kind of social lubricant. The term also refers to the diffusion and adoption of coffee as a highly popular stimulant by a culture.

The history and formation of cultures around coffee and coffee house dates back to fourteenth century Turkey. Coffee houses in the western world over the time have become social hubs for artistic and intellectual interaction. Today coffee houses can be found in almost all major cities of the world, where elements of coffee culture can be seen more or less in the same traditional social styles.

Popular culture - Popular culture refers to the aggregation of totality of ideas, perspectives, attitudes, images and other phenomenon that permeates the everyday lives of the members of a society, especially those heavily influenced by mass media. The study of such culture is of great importance for national and international marketers. The most common pop culture examples are – Movies, Music, TV, Sports, News, Politics, Fashion/Clothes, Technology, and Slang, etc. Popular culture are often termed as trivial and dumb as it finds consensual acceptance by the mainstream. As a result, pop culture is often despised and criticized by non – mainstream groups like religious groups which regard any such pop culture as superficial, consumerist, sensational or even corrupt. To them a pop culture is often a symbol of a dawning of the society morals and damaging to traditional ways of living.

Cosmopolitan culture - Cosmopolitanism is an ideology that portrays all human beings belong to a single community and must share similar moral and economic values. Therefore, in cosmopolitanism, a culture may be based on an inclusive morality, a shared economic relationship or a political thinking which is beyond national boundaries. One example of cosmopolitanism is the existence of a set of globe trotters in all major cities of the world who share similar political, moral and economic thoughts irrespective of their nationality and prefer similar lifestyles wherever they are located. They find any major city in the world homely as they are able to use similar resources, products and infrastructure whichever city they are in. For international marketers, such cosmopolitan cultures are very important as they are able to produce and market cosmopolitan products which can be sold in the same form in several countries of the world. For example *'United Colors of Benetton'* is a clothing company which caters to people of such cosmopolitan societies throughout the world selling a similar range of collection of clothes globally.

In addition, national cultures have been studied based on certain cultural dimensions by several social researchers. In recent times, a lot of research work has been done on cultural dimensions. Most of these work aims at comparing organizational cultures and national cultures from different perspectives, making it easier to map human behavior on this planet in simpler terms.

While there is no denying the fact that the concept of national culture may be fraught with generalizations due to the possible existence of cultures within cultures i.e. subcultures. Nevertheless concept of nation cultures has made the understanding of world cultures comparatively easier, especially from a commercial point of view. There are inherent assumptions of the existence of common national cultures. Based on these assumptions, researchers have been able to suggest several cultural models which have made cultural comparisons easier. Moreover, the existence of so many cultural variables of the elements has made it very difficult to carry out cultural comparison especially in an international context. Therefore, many researchers have categorized cultures using so called cultural dimensions models along with the assumptions related to national cultures. These concepts form the basis of the thought process of the authors of this book.

Some of the classical studies on national cultural differences are discussed in the following paragraphs for more clarity and as a foundation of the construct of this book.

Cultural dimensions and cultural differences

Cultural characteristics and differences can be studied on several lines. One of the most important and the earliest studies in modern times, done to understand cultural differences among international cultures, is the 'five dimension model' of cultural differences as suggested by *Hofstede* (1980, 1983,1987, 1991 and 1997) [14]. Five culture dimensions suggested by *Hofstede*, have contributed enormously to a deeper understanding of the theories and dynamics of cross cultural management based on these categories of mental programming. The variables identified in his research assumed that all reactions in working relationship or production of behavior, thereof, will be reflected at a workplace assimilating the social, organizational and personal 'values and beliefs'.

The reason *Hofstede* focused on individual countries for his study was his belief that differences and similarities in cultural patterns were easily identifiable and meaningful at the nation-state level. He attributed the cultures measured in each nation-state to its 'historical roots' and certain 'mechanisms in societies that permit the maintenance of stability in cultural patterns across generations' [15]. *Hofstede* continues by declaring that institutions 'reinforce the societal norms and the ecological conditions that led to their establishment'.

Trompenaar's (1997) seven dimensions model of national cultural differences, specifies more layers to explain national cultural differences [16] –

1. Universalism versus particularism (What is more important, rules or relationships?);
2. Individualism vs. collectivism (communitarianism) (Do we function in a group or as individuals?);
3. Neutral vs. emotional (Do we display our emotions?);
4. Specific vs. diffuse (How separate we keep our private and working lives);
5. Achievement vs. ascription (Do we have to prove ourselves to receive status or is it given to us?);
6. Sequential vs. synchronic (Do we do things one at a time or several things at once?);
7. Internal vs. external control (Do we control our environment or are we controlled by it?).

The work on this model is based on 1000 + corporate training programs done by the researcher. He tried to understand whether the management concepts learnt in *American* B-Schools can be used to train people of different *European* countries. The researcher indicates from his experiences that the concepts vary from country to country. Therefore, international managers need to work on several premises. These premises emanate from local sensitivities which vary from one country to another.

The researcher concluded there are visible and invisible ways in which local culture impacts the organization. When you compare same global organization within several countries you will visibly find the organization across nations are not different and therefore 'local culture' free. But when you go deeper you find that is not true. There are invisible factors that differentiate same organization in one country to another due to the impact of local cultures. These suggestions by the author's hint at the inquiry of cross cultural group interaction process in multicultural teams, especially in terms of 'comfort of local cultures with foreign cultures' to inquire about those invisible factors.

GLOBE (Global Leadership and Organizational Behavior Effectiveness) study empirically established nine cultural dimensions that make it possible to capture the similarities and differences in norms, values, beliefs and practices, among societies. Using these cultural dimensions, in the way similar to the work of *Hofstede*, this study also identified different cultural groups across the world, which are likely to show similar cultures. GLOBE studied the preferred leadership styles in different cultural clusters and concluded studies on the six styles of leaders who are the preferred by each cluster group, but the level of preference of the latter style vary from cluster to cluster. For example 'performance oriented leadership style' is highly preferred in *Anglo* and *Germanic* cultures, while 'self or group – protective leader style' is least preferred in these cultures. These differences in preferred leadership styles across cultures further reinforce the need to study intercultural comfort among multicultural team members at workplaces. This research also gives new insights into the way forward for the theme of the book, especially with respect to the development of the questionnaire and a selection of respondent and destination cultures.

Cultural competence

One of the concepts of cross cultural management, which is closely related to the concept of intercultural comfort or CFC, is 'intercultural competence'. Cultural competence refers to the ability of individuals to interact effectively with persons of different cultures. Such abilities can be developed through broadening one's worldview, knowledge of other cultures, cross cultural training, developing the right attitude towards cultural differences. Developing cultural competency can result in improving the ability to interact, understand and communicate effectively with people across cultures[17].

Organizational culture and cross cultural management

The discomfort among employees of different cultural backgrounds may also be the result of differences in terms of 'cultural competence' of a person of one culture to understand an alien culture. A basic requirement of desired cultural competence has five dimensions [18] to it. These are:

1. Level of empathy to other cultures,
2. Knowledge of other cultures,
3. Self confidence (knowledge of one's own desires, expectations, strengths and weaknesses),
4. Cultural Identity (Knowledge of one's own culture),

5.   Emotional Stability.

Due to obvious variations in these five elements from one culture to another culture, propensity to feel comfortable with a person with a foreign cultural background may vary from one culture to another. Such variation may also vary among different combinations of pairs of employees of different background interacting with each other. The level of such comfort of one culture with another can also emerge from individual traits like – being, cultural savvy, astuteness, appreciative, literate, adaptable, having expertise, competent, aware, intelligent and understanding [19]. The concept gives new insights into the organizational cultures and cross cultural management at multicultural workplaces.

Conclusion

What appears from the above discussion, is that the term 'culture' has been a subject of intense debate and discussion for a very long time and refers to deferring societal behavior from several perspectives. In the modern times, term 'culture' has assumed great significance and a topic of deeper study as it has come to denote the behavior of the people of the organizations which may operate across borders.

Due to its rising importance term 'culture' has acquired a larger status of wide attention from sociologists, anthropologists, academicians, researchers, politicians, social activists and practitioners among others. A lot has already been researched about the cultures of the world and their differences. Still the topic remains in its infancy and not thoroughly understood and confidently managed specially in multinational organizations.

Suggested questions of discussion

1.   Why do cultures vary from one country to another country or one region to another region?
2.   What are the common elements of cultures which describe a culture of a nation? Discuss with examples.
3.   What is the concept of 'national culture'? Are there any subcultures within certain national cultures? Discuss.
4.   What is the concept of Semiotics of Culture? Discuss with examples.
5.   Do you think 'level of comfort' of national culture with foreign cultures, varies among different nations? Discuss with examples.
6.   What is Cultural Competence? How does it differ from 'level of

CFC'? Discuss.

7. What are the different approaches of categorizing the common types of cultures? Discuss with examples.
8. What are the different approaches of comparing world cultures?
9. How do cultural dimensional models help in understanding cultural differences among nations? Discuss.
10. What is Group-Grid theory? Discuss the concept with examples.

Notes

1. Emmitt, S., Gorse, C.A. (2007). *Communication Construction Teams*

2. Shenkar, O. & Zeira, Y. (1992). Role conflict and role ambiguity of CEO's in international joint ventures'. *Journal of International Business Studies* 23 (1), 55–75.

3. Ochieng, E.G. & Price, A.D.F. (2009). Managing cross-cultural communication in multicultural construction project teams: The case of Kenya and UK. *International Journal of Project Management.*

4. Dainty, A.R.J., Green, S. & Bagilhole, B. (2007) *People and Culture in Construction. Taylor and Francis Group*, Oxon.

5. Pearson, J.C. & Nelson, P.E. (2003). *Human Communication.* McGraw-Hill, New York.

6. Taylor, E.B. (1871), *Primitive culture: researches into the development of mythology, philosophy, religion, art and custom.* 2 vols. London, Johney Murray

7. Nine-Curt, Carmen Judith. (1984) *Non-verbal Communication in Puerto Rico. Cambridge*, Massachusetts.

8. Denboba, D.L. et al. (1998) Reducing health disparities through cultural competence. *Journal of Health Education* 29 (5, Supplement): S47-53

9. Chamberlain, SP (2005). Recognizing and responding to cultural differences in the education of culturally and linguistically diverse learners. *Intervention in School & Clinic*, 40(4), p.195-211.

10. Cicero, Marcus Tullius (45 BC), *Tusculanes (Tusculan Disputations).* pp. II, 15.

11. O'Neil, D. (2006). "*Processes of Change*".

12. Pringle, H. (1998). The Slow Birth of Agriculture. *Science* 282: 1446

13. Geletkanycz, M. A. (1997). The salience of 'culture's consequences': The effects of cultural values on top executive commitment to the status quo. *Strategic Management Journal*, 18(5), p.615-634.

14. Hofstede, G. (1980). *Culture's consequences: International differences in work-related values.* Beverly Hills, CA: Sage.

    Hofstede, G. (1983). The Cultural Relativity of Organizational Practices and Theories, *Journal of International Business Studies*, 14, 1983

    Hofstede, Geert (1987). "The Applicability of McGregor's Theories in South

East Asia," *Journal of Management Development*, Vol. 6, No. 3, 9-18.

Hoststede, G. (1991). *Culture and organizations: Software of the mind.* London: McGraw-Hill.

Hofstede, G. (1997). *Cultures and Organizations: Software of the Mind.* New York: McGraw Hill.

15. Hofstede, G. (2001). *Culture's consequences: Comparing values, behaviors, institutions, and organizations across nations.* Thousand Oaks, CA: Sage.

16. Trompenaars F. & Hampden-Turner, C. (1997). *Riding the waves of culture: Understanding diversity in global business (2nd Ed.).* New York: McGraw-Hill.

17. Campinha-Bacote, J. (1991). *The Process of Cultural Competence: A Culturally Competent Model of Care.* Wyoming, Ohio: Transcultural C.A.R.E Associates

18. Cross, T., Bazron, B., Dennis, K. & Isaacs, M., (1989). *Towards A Culturally Competent System of Care*, Volume I. Washington, DC: Georgetown University Child Development Center, CASSP Technical Assistance Center.

19. Selmeski, BR (2007). *Military cross-cultural competence: Core concepts and individual development.* Kingston: Royal Military College of *Canada* Centre for Security, Armed Forces, & Society.

Online resources for this chapter, available at:
http://www.vijeshjain.com/books/multinational-workplaces/resources/chapter-2

3. CULTURAL DIFFERNCES, CULTURAL DIMENSIONS AND CFC

The concept of cultural differences has been discussed in detail in this chapter, particularly as understood by topologies of *Hofstede, Trompenaars, GLOBE Study* and *Group – Grid Theory*. It is argued that these topologies give a strong direction to the understanding of the concept of 'level of CFC'. The concept of CFC has also been described in the context of organizational behavior in this chapter. At the same time 'cultural differences' have been discussed in the context of organizations and organizational identity. Somewhere the introduction of the concept of 'level of CFC' at workplaces emerges as the central theme of this chapter.

Comparative international studies to record cultural differences are broadly based on certain popular cultural models, so called 'onion models' or 'multi-layered models' or 'multi-dimensions models'. Most popular among these are those suggested by *Hofstede* (1980, 1991), *Fons Trompenaars* (1997), *Shalom Schwartz* (1994, 2006), GLOBE study (*House, R, et al,* 2001), *Smith* (1995), *Inglehart* (1997) and others[1]. These differences emerge from several factors such as ethnical differences, ethical differences, geographical differences, moral differences, historical differences, political differences, linguistic differences and religious differences. In the cases of business communication between persons of different national cultural backgrounds, such differences can play an important role which may manifest into certain degree of friction, discomfort and inability to appreciate 'these mutual differences and different ways of thinking of persons of foreign cultures'[2], potentially affecting the performance of the project teams[3].

In global organizations these cultural differences are prominently visible and have to be dealt with carefully. Using the concept of national cultures[4], it is possible to study workplace cultural differences with a certain clarity. However, more tools are needed to study the differences of intercultural discomfort. The study of such variations of level of CFC among different cultures can be very useful to manage diversity.

Currently, organizations are harvesting strategic advantages of cultural diversity in project teams[5]. Such strategic advantages, either to profit and non-profit organizations may include improved human resource management, enriched team performance, better change management, better headquarter – subsidiary relations, and better talent management, among others. The study of such differences can also be very useful, for instance, in protecting international students and/or immigrant workers, for instance, who are more likely to experience frequent cultural shocks when working or studying in a country which is distinct in culture from their native countries. Such studies can be used to train them to better adapt to host cultures, to appreciate these and blend with these, instead of living with fear, hatred, inferiority complex and living with bicultural identities.

International managers would also benefit by mitigating these risks, and such understanding would be very good for international business performance of multicultural work teams. This book proposes that 'level of intercultural comfort' is an independent cultural dimension and is unique to different national cultures. Cultural behavior of this kind can be distinctive to national cultures and generalization can be useful for this purpose, if done in international context when comparisons among countries are useful[6]. Therefore, using 'empirical comparative cross cultural study', it may be possible to map the 'variable propensity' of 'intercultural comfort' among multicultural team members, coming from different distinct national cultural backgrounds.

However, it would require a large amount of resources and time for cross cultural researchers to map all such cultural pairs globally. In later chapters of this book, authors have described the attempts to perform some of these comparisons with a limited set of cultural pairs, using research data from a set of multinational employees from different national cultures.

'Intercultural comfort' is often confused with different cultural concepts related to 'cultural competence' or 'cultural distance'. But the concept of 'intercultural comfort' appears to be different from these concepts. While cultural competence refers to the level of awareness of a society about alien cultures of the world and about their ability to develop such awareness, it does not necessarily explain their actual reaction to other cultures in diverse kinds of encounters. Such reactions seem to be a function of several factors which are discussed in different sections of this book through the concept of 'level of CFC'. The concept of cultural distance is discussed in this chapter and is distinct from CFC in terms of its scope and context.

In addition, there are several cultural dimensions suggested in different comparative cultural studies, which may seem to explain the phenomenon of 'intercultural comfort'. However, none of these researches have been able to clearly define the phenomenon. Many of these studies and models do explain somewhat indirectly, the reaction of persons of local culture to their interaction with persons of foreign cultural background. However, such explanations are not complete, qualitative in nature, explain general reactions and do not touch upon 'intercultural comfort' among specific national culture to another specific culture or so called, 'national cultural pairs'. This book tries to explain such 'intercultural comfort' more directly, discretely, quantitatively.

In later chapters, CFC among cultural pairs is also discussed using a set of empirical research data. These cultural models often plot dimensions such as - orientation to time, space, communication, competitiveness, power etc., as complimentary pairs of attributes. Different cultures are placed on a continuum between the extremes associated with these pairs. Some of the most popular contemporary models of defining world cultures are discussed in following paragraphs.

Hofstede's cultural dimensions

In 1980, *Geert Hofstede* published, 'Culture's Consequences', a monumental work that represented more than a decade of research. In his book, along with subsequent editions, *Hofstede* established that 'people carry 'mental programs' that are developed in the family in early childhood and reinforced in school and organizations', assuming that 'these mental programs contain a component of national culture' [7]. He categorized the differences in mental programming by identifying four cultural dimensions[8]. *Hofstede* and *Bond* (1984)[9] later identified a fifth dimension after research on behaviors of *Chinese* professionals. These five cultural dimensions[10] have contributed enormously to a deeper understanding of the theories and dynamics of cross cultural management based on these categories of mental programming.

The variables identified in these researches assumed that all reactions in working relationship or production of behavior, thereof, will be reflected at a workplace assimilating the social, organizational and personal 'values and beliefs' [11]. The reason *Hofstede* focused on individual countries for his study was his belief that differences and similarities in cultural patterns were more easily identifiable and meaningful at the national level. He attributed the cultures measured in each nation-state to 'historical roots' and certain 'mechanisms in societies that result into a stability in cultural patterns across generations'. *Hofstede* continued by declaring that institutions 'reinforce the societal norms and the ecological conditions that lead to their establishment' [7] (see figure 3.1).

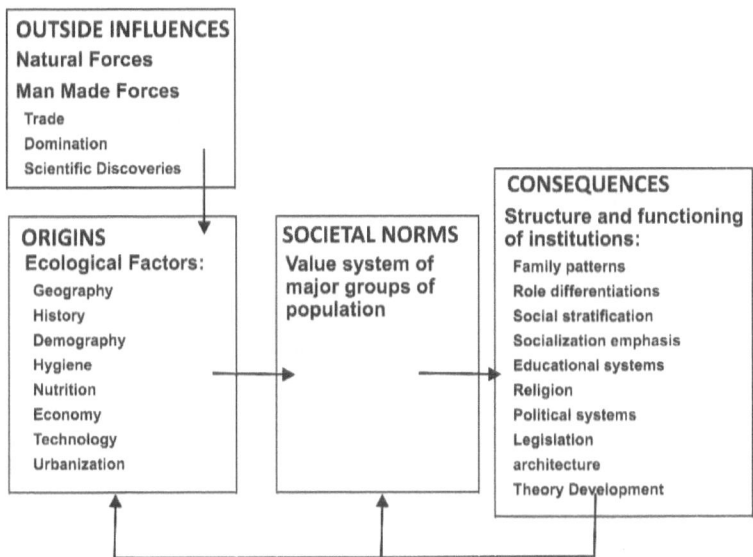

Figure 3.1: Conceptual scheme of *Hofstede's* model

Hofstede argued that a change in one institution would not have a great impact on the national culture because people, as the bearers of that culture, would 'smooth' the institution's structures and its methods of functioning until they 'are again adapted to the societal norms' [7, 12].

Hofstede's explanation of reaction of local cultures to foreign cultures

Hofstede offered his judgment on how host societies react to the arrival of foreigners[7]. According to him, the reaction consists of three steps.

1. In step 1, the locals are curious about how different the foreigners are (i.e., the 'zoo' effect).

2. In next step is ethnocentrism. Its occurrence leads to the locals perceiving their cultures as superior to those of the foreigners. And

3. Last step, which takes, the longer than the others to be reached – and which, in fact, may never be reached in some societies – is 'polycentrism', where locals evaluate the foreigner as having different standards because they are different.

In the last step, there is no judgment on the part of the locals whether the foreigners' standards are better or worse than their own; it is merely that they are different.

Guessing from these accounts of *Hofstede*, in a market economy, businesses are expected to assume a polycentric view to better serve local and foreign customers, thus enabling them to adapt their products and services to the needs of cross cultural customers. This could allow them to gain a competitive advantage in saturated local markets. The above accounts of *Hofstede* gave a better view of the intercultural group process and help identify possible CFC variables to be used for devising a framework for quantitative investigation into the phenomenon of intercultural comfort at multinational workplaces.

Trompenaar's dimensions

Trompenaars and *Hampden-Turner* (1997) [13] adopted another kind of an onion-like model of culture. According to this model, culture is made up of basic assumptions at the core level. These 'basic assumptions' are somewhat similar to 'values' in the *Hofstede's* model. Accordingly 'culture' is the way people solve their problem and reconcile their dilemmas. The authors of this model use eight dimensions of their model namely-

1. Universalism vs. Particularism (what is more important - rules or relationships?),

2. Individualism vs. Communitarianism (do we function in a group or as an individual?),

3. Neutral vs. Emotional (do we display our emotions or keep them to ourselves?),

4. Specific vs. Diffuse (how far do we get involved?),

5. Achievement vs. Ascription (do we have to prove ourselves to gain status or is it given to us just because we are a part of a structure?),

6. Attitude to Time, (past, present, future - orientation),

7. Sequential time vs. Synchronic time (do we do things one at a time or several things at once?) and

8. Internal vs. External Orientation (do we aim to control our environment or adjust to it?).

The work on above model is based on 1000 + corporate training programs done by the researcher and tries to understand whether the management concepts learnt in *American* B-Schools can be used to train people of different *European* countries. The researcher of the above model indicated from their experience that the concepts vary from country to country. Therefore, international managers need to work on several premises. These premises emanate from local sensitivities which vary from one country to another. The researcher concluded from these accounts, there are visible and invisible ways in which local culture impacts the organization. When you compare same global organization within several countries you will visibly find the organization across nations are not different and therefore 'local culture' free. But when you go deeper you find that is not true. There are invisible factors that differentiate same organization in one country to another due to the impact of local cultures. And therefore as the researcher concluded it does not matter if the hierarchies in international project teams are similar from country to country what these hierarchies mean to local cultures may be different and therefore may have an impact on the performance.

These suggestions give certain basis to understand the intercultural comfort among international project teams as well as to identify observed and latent variables for devising the CFC model.

GLOBE study

A different perspective has been taken by GLOBE (Global Leadership and Organizational Behavior Effectiveness) research project that focused on the relationships between societal culture, organizational culture and leadership. GLOBE built on *Hofstede's* (1980)[14] and others' [13] work and through its research, surfaced 10 cultural clusters representing core dimensions from 62 cultures around the world. GLOBE used the term 'societal culture' instead of 'national culture' to 'indicate the complexity of the culture concept and in several instances it sampled two subcultures from a single nation' [15]. A working assumption of the GLOBE project was that many countries have multiple, large subcultures within their borders[16], which many times expand beyond the borders. Efforts were directed toward drawing representative samples that were comparable to dominant forces that shape culture, including 'history, language, politics, and religion' [16], and they sampled from more than one subculture in large countries.

Despite these efforts, due to the nature of the study, it had limited capacity to discern subgroups within societies[17]. However the study diverted the attention of social scientists from nation – state cultural approach to sub – culture or regional culture approach where geographical considerations were limited. Therefore, cultural groups identified in the GLOBE study comprised of subcultures and regional cultures representing several geographically distant cultures classified in same cultural groupings. GLOBE studied the preferred leadership styles in different cultural clusters and concluded studies on the six styles of leaders are the most preferred by each cluster group, but the level of preference of the latter style vary from cluster to cluster. For example 'performance oriented leadership style' is highly preferred in *Anglo* and *Germanic* cultures, while 'self or group – protective leader style' is least preferred in these cultures.

These findings reinforced the saying that 'preferred leadership styles lies in the beholder's eyes'. This, on the same note, should mean that intercultural comfort among cross cultural comfort dynamics should behave in somewhat similar manner. Therefore GLOBE study is a significant step forward in better understanding of the cultural dimensions and cultural world groupings and also may serve as an important basis to understand the cultural landscape of the societal comfort of local cultures with foreigners and foreign cultures.

Group - grid theory

Group - grid is a 'cultural theory of risk perception'. It is a cultural model developed by anthropologists *Mary Douglas* (1978), *Michael Thompson* (1990), and *Steve Rayner* [18], with contributions by political scientists *Aaron Wildavsky* and *Richard Ellis*, and others. This cultural theory asserted that structures of social organizations endow individuals with perceptions that reinforce those structures in competition against alternative ones. It becomes an important area of understanding in multinational firms operating globally and promoting cross cultural teams.

Another reason this theory was designed was to show how native rituals and practices were relevant to modern society and therefore how they affect organizational cultures. The model is a 2 X 2 matrix model with group and grid dimensions (See figure 3.2).

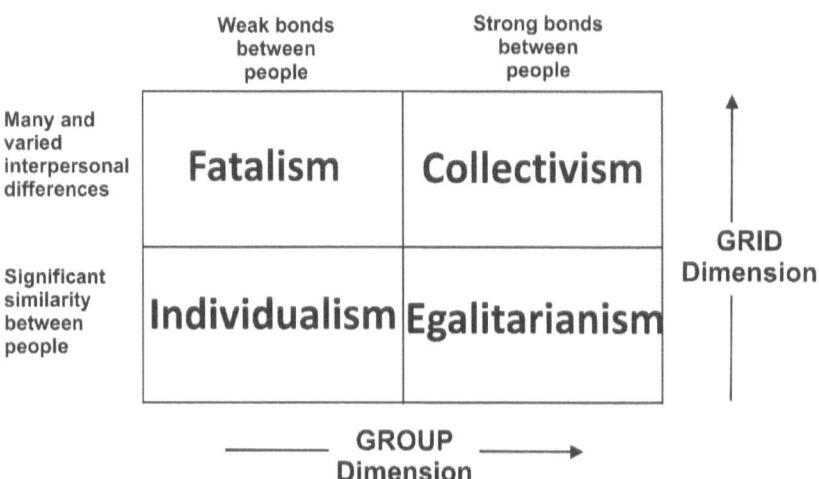

Figure 3.2: Group -grid theory

The group dimension indicates how strongly people are bonded together.

At one end of 'low group' effect, there are distinct and separated individuals, probably with common reasons to be together, though with less of a sense of unity and connection. At the other end of 'high group' effect, people have a connected sense of identity, relating more deeply and intimately to each other. They spend more time together and have relatively stable relationships. When people forms bonded group together, they found laws are more easily defined and implemented. On the other hand, for society to survive in an environment of weaker interpersonal bonds and lesser central control, individuals must necessarily display self-restraint. From a management perspective, 'low group' is not understood to manage resources well, whilst high group does.

The grid dimension demonstrates how different people are positioned in the group and how they take on different roles and responsibilities. At one end of this spectrum, i.e. 'low grid' effect people are relatively homogeneous in their work, activity and abilities. It is relatively easy for them to interchange roles. This makes them less dependent on one another. At the other end with 'high grid' effect, there are distinctively defined roles and positions with specialization and different accountability incorporated in the groups. There are also different degrees of entitlement, depending on the position one holds and there may well be a different balance of exchange between and across individuals. This makes it advantageous to share and organize together. From a management perspective, 'low grid' does not manage needs, whilst 'high grid' does.

The group – grid theory postulates through its matrix model that primarily there are predominantly four types of cultures in this world (see figure 3.2 and 3.3). These are named as:

1. Fatalism – Indicating high grid, but low group effect.
2. Collectivism – Indicating high grid as well as high group effect.
3. Individualism – Indicating low grid as well as low group effect.
4. Egalitarianism – Indicating low grid, but high group effect.

The above cultural theory has also tried to explain, inter societal conflicts, in terms of 4 or 5 ways of life and how they interact with each other and therefore how they affect organizational cultures. These are:

Fatalism

According to this theory fatalism occurs due to many and varied interpersonal differences coupled with weaker bonds between members of the society, resulting in a fatalistic environment characterized by isolating members and subordinates having a lack of trust with each other. There is little freedom of choice among members of society. Members rely on the intervention of 'government, god and fate' in their life for improvement and growth. Environment in such culture is generally business unfriendly. Companies are typically taken over by large corporations or remain in financial turmoil. Such societies are believed to be unable to manage needs as well as the resources of the society.

Hierarchies (Collectivism)

These cultures emerge from a strong bond between members of the society, but having many and varied interpersonal differences. However, relationships are orderly and inequality is normal, which is required to preserve the system. Collective prevails over individual and loyalty is rewarded. Business environment in companies is typically autocratic, bureaucratic and monopolistic in nature. These types of societies are able to manage resources, but are unable to manage needs.

Individualism

Individualistic cultures, according to group-grid model, emerge from significant similarities between people but weaker bonds between people. These types of societies are characterized by highly mobile members who accept inequalities based on the concept of 'survival of the fittest'. Gaps between the rich and the poor may be quite high. They believe in market culture and the supremacy of the customer. Business environment in such cultures is typically flexible, risk taking and motivating. Individual performance is celebrated and rewarded. Corporations in such societies are generally oligopolistic and thrive in market through strategic alliances and using competitive networks. These societies are believed to be able to manage both needs as well as resources.

Egalitarian

Such cultures emerge from significant similarities among members as well as strong bonds between people. However, relationships are voluntary in nature. There exists a 'wall of virtue' between 'in group' and 'out group' which separates society from outside. So while members are strongly bonded together, there is no scope of hierarchies due to equal status. It poses a great challenge to the preservation of the system, resulting into no legitimacy to any leadership. Most such societies are by 'non-profit' nature which actually preserves the system to some extent. Most such societies are socially responsible and believe in charismatic leadership. It is observed that such societies are able to manage needs, but unable to manage resources.

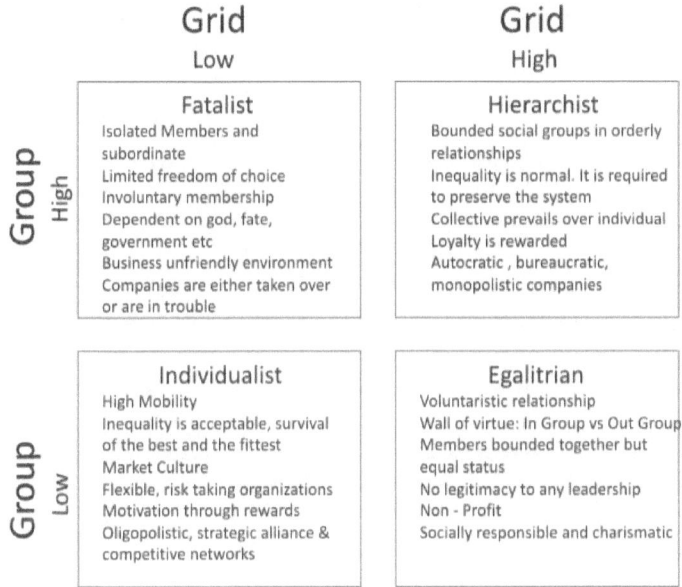

Figure 3.3: Typical characteristics of different cultures of Group-Grid

There is another fifth type of culture, according to group – grid theory. This is called Hermit culture. The members of this culture like to live in seclusion and interact with other culture only when essential.

Most of these research works are inconclusive though. There are a number of gaps and contradictions in those situations.

Theory of cultural distance

Irrespective of the way culture is defined, differences in various elements of culture, e.g., language, social structure, religions, ways and standards of living, values, etc., result into something called 'cultural distance' (CD) and this distance is larger when two cultures are quite different[19]. An important manifestation of the concept of 'cultural distance' is how one culture perceives behavior of the other. If the CD is greater, it is possible that people from one country, while on a visit or to settle in another country, may find it quite uncomfortable to interact with people of the host country or vice versa[20]. *Triandis* (1994)[19] suggested that one major reason for such behavior or feeling is that most of us are having 'ethnocentric' approach by default. In this approach we tend to view our own behavioral norms as more correct and those of others as not so correct or worse as wrong. This suggests that when people from different cultural backgrounds interact with each other, such aggregation may create a sense of discomfort among the members due to perceived differences in behavioral norms or cultural conditioning.

These incidences of the lower 'level of CFC' during interpersonal communication with people of the host country is likely to be even lesser in an environment that is not too familiar to the visitor, more so for the immigrants or visitors from low context cultures. It has even been claimed that in certain cases of possible extreme discomfort of this type, even global conflicts could occur [21]. This view has also been supported by the discussions and researches involving the high-low context dichotomy[20]. Literature dealing with immigration and expatriate managers, and acculturation [22, 23, 24], also discusses similar phenomenon. It is suggested that if a CD is less, the visitor is likely to feel more comfortable with the host culture. This discomfort may increase due to differences in languages, beliefs, attitudes etc.

Origins of the theory of cultural distance

Concept of the CD was first found in FDI (foreign direct investment) literature, most often in the form of an index compiled by *Kogut* and *Singh* (1988)[25] and *Hofstede's* (1980)[1] cultural dimensions. In FDI literature, CD has been explained to have three applications.

1) First relate to explanation of location of market investment by multinational firms.
2) The second explanation of CD has been the choice of the mode of entry and
3) A third application relates to variable success, failure and overall performance of MNE affiliates in the international market place and success or failure of cross cultural teams in international projects [3].

In the third application, the CD has been explained to be an obstacle to the overall success of cross cultural teams in international projects. For example CD limits the ability of multinational firms to generate profits from new domain entries in the global markets[26]. For example, it is found that *US* affiliates whose foreign associates or partners came from culturally distance cultures were more likely to fail [27]. In other studies, it is found that CD decreased international joint ventures (IJV) longevity[28]. On the different side there are studies which found no direct effect of CD on multinational firm's performance. For example, *Johnson, Cullen* and *Sakano*[29] (1991) reported that 'cultural congruence' among IJV partners has no effect on the *Japanese* partner's perception of success or failure. *Similarly Park* and *Ungson* (1997)[30] found that a larger CD was associated with lower rates of IJV failure. However, *Shenker* (2001)[3] suggests that these mixed results of CD effect may be the result of weakness of conceptual and methodological properties of the CD construct which are neither supported by logic nor by empirical results.

Criticism of existing cultural models

While most of the cross cultural studies mentioned above provide great insights into the inquiry of mapping CFC, there are a few criticisms of these studies which are important to mention here. In this book, efforts have been made that the concepts of cross cultural management, are presented in a manner so that these are understood in the context of these criticisms. Readers are also advised to understand the limitations of the theme of this book.

One of the important criticisms about above mentioned cross cultural studies relates to the outcome of these studies vis-a-vis their main objectives. While the important objectives of cross cultural studies have been developing an understanding of cultural differences which can help team managers to promote cohesive work culture and peace among employees of different cultural background, these studies have often been criticized for creating stereotypes rather than promoting understanding among distinct cultural groups[31]. *Osland and Bird* (2000)[32] refer to these stereotypes as 'sophisticated stereotypes' which are generated out of cross cultural research, training and theoretical concepts. They further postulate that this phenomenon could also be the result of the differences of own world view of the researchers from different countries depending upon their native cultural conditioning.

Madison (2006) [33] has criticized the cross cultural competence training for its tendency to simplify the processes of migration and cross cultural management into stages and phases. Other studies have questioned the concept of nation character and cultural dimensions to study people and culture in organizations[34]. Another weakness of above theories has been the inability to transcend the tendency to equalize culture with the concept of the nation state. A nation state is a political unit consisting of an independent state, inhabited predominantly by people sharing similar culture, history, and languages. In real life, cultures do not have strict physical boundaries and borders like nation states. Its expression and even inherent beliefs can be a product of many possible relationships and combinations as we move across geographical distances.

There is another criticism in the field that such approaches are out of phase with global business realities of today, with transnational companies facing the challenges of the management of multicultural project teams and global knowledge networks, interacting and collaborating across the national borders, using new communication technologies. *Nigel Holden* (2001)[35] suggests an alternative approach, which acknowledges the growing complexity of inter- and intra-organizational connections and identities, and proposes theoretical concepts to think about organizations and multiple cultures in a global business context.

In spite of several shortcomings and criticisms faced by the *Hofstede's* model and similar other popular models, some of these models specially that of *Hofstede's* are very much favored by trainers and researchers. Therefore, most of these researches support the idea of making a deeper study of the nature of interaction among local cultures and foreign cultures at multinational workplaces especially in the context of intercultural comfort. The accounts given in this book therefore take a different approach for its construct which is based on the common perception of persons of different cultural backgrounds on how they would choose or prefer to work and associate with persons of other cultural backgrounds.

Conclusion

The chapter discussed a set of important research on the cultural differences and their implications on the element of cultures which may have an impact on the phenomenon of 'level of CFC' among employees working at multinational and multicultural workplaces. These researches provided a strong direction and clues to move forward to the search of a suitable cross cultural model which could help understand the landscape of the variation of 'level of comfort' among employees of different cultural background and to help make comparison of these differences.

Suggested questions for discussion

1) What are the so called 'Onion Models' of cultural differences among national cultures? Discuss with examples.

2) How have the most popular cultural dimension models postulated in recent times improved the understanding of social scientists about world cultures? What is their true relevance to cross cultural management? Discuss with examples.

3) Discuss the perspective of *Hofstede* on - how do host cultures react to the arrival of foreigners? Do you agree or disagree with his explanation? Why? Discuss with examples.

4) Compare cultural dimensions of *Hofstede* and *Trompenaar's* model. Discuss the merits and demerits of these two models vis-a-vis each other.

5) Discuss the major differences in the conceptual framework of GLOBE study when compared with other similar earlier researches.

6) What is the basic concept of Group – Grid Theory? Does it explain the cultural differences across nations? How relevant is the theory in the present context? Discuss

7) Why is the theory of cultural distance so controversial with differing perspectives of different social critics? Discuss.

8) What are the main criticisms of the popular cultural models? Did you really think we already understand the phenomenon of cultural differences across nations and their impact on organizations? Discuss.

Notes

1. Hofstede, G. (1980). *Culture's consequences: International differences in work-related values.* Beverly Hills, CA: Sage.

   Hoststede, G. (1991). *Culture and organizations: Software of the mind.* London: McGraw-Hill.

   Trompenaars F. & Hampden-Turner, C. (1997). *Riding the waves of culture: Understanding diversity in global business* (2nd Ed.). New York: McGraw-Hill.

   Schwartz, SH (2006). Value orientations: Measurement, antecedents and consequences across nations. In R. Jowell, C. Roberts, R. Fitzgerald, & G. Eva (Eds.) *Measuring attitudes cross-nationally - lessons from the European Social Survey.* London: Sage

   House, R., Javidan, M. & Dorfman, PW (2001). *Project GLOBE: An introduction. Applied Psychology: An International Review,* 50(4), 489-505.

   Smith, PB and Peterson, MF (1995). "Beyond Value Comparisons: Sources Used to Give Meaning to Management Work Events in

Twenty-Nine Countries." Paper presented at the annual meeting of the *Academy of Management*, Vancouver, Canada.

Inglehart, R. (1997). *Modernization and Post-Modernization: Cultural, Economic, and Political Change in 43 Societies*. Princeton, N.J.: Princeton University Press, 1997

2. Shenkar, O. & Zeira, Y. (1992). Role conflict and role ambiguity of CEO's in international joint ventures'. *Journal of International Business Studies* 23 (1), 55–75.

3. Shenker, O. (2001). Cultural distance revisited: Towards a more rigorous conceptualization and measurement of Cultural Differences., *Journal of International Business Studies*; Third Quarter; 32, 3; ABI/INFORM Global, pg. 519

4. Hofstede, G. (1980). *Culture's consequences: International differences in work-related values*. Beverly Hills, CA: Sage.

Hofstede, G. (1983). The Cultural Relativity of Organizational Practices and Theories, *Journal of International Business Studies*, 14, 1983

Hofstede, G. (1984). *Culture's consequences: International differences in work-related values*. Newbury Park, CA: Sage

5. Love, A. (2010). "Diversity as a Strategic Advantage", *Business Week*. Web article. Retrieved from

http://www.businessweek.com/managing/content/may2010/ca20100513_748402.htm on 2014-12-20

6. Hoststede, G. (1991). *Culture and organizations: Software of the mind*. London: McGraw-Hill.

7. Hofstede, G. (2001). *Culture's consequences: Comparing values, behaviors, institutions, and organizations across nations*. Thousand Oaks, CA: Sage.

8. The work of Geert *Hofstede* on over 100,000 professionals which were covered from 50 countries in three regions between 1967 and 1973 propounded the theory of *Cultural Dimensions* to understand cross cultural issues.

9. Hofstede, G. & Bond, M.H. (1984). "*Hofstede*'s Culture Dimensions: An Independent Validation Using Rokeach's Value Survey." *Journal of Cross-Cultural Psychology*, 15(4): 417-433

10. The five dimensions *Hofstede* used to distinguish between national cultures are- 1) Power distance, which measures the extent to which members of society accept how power is distributed equally or unequally in that society. 2) Individualism, tells how people individually perceive themselves and their immediate family only in contrast

with Collectivism, where people belong to in-groups (families, clans or organizations) who look after them in exchange for loyalty. The dominant values of 3) Masculinity, focusing on achievement and material success are contrasted with those of Femininity, which focuses on caring for others and a quality of life. 4) Uncertainty avoidance, measures the extent to which people feel threatened by uncertainty and ambiguity and try to avoid these situations. 5) Confucian dynamism - this Long-term versus Short-term orientation measured the fostering of virtues related to the past, i.e., respect for tradition, importance of keeping face and thrift.

11. The same assumption hold true for the current research too

12. However, *Hofstede* does not fully consider the impact on local cultures by high levels of immigration over a long period of time.

13. Trompenaars F. & Hampden-Turner, C. (1997). *Riding the waves of culture: Understanding diversity in global business* (2nd Ed.). New York: McGraw-Hill.

14. Hofstede, G. (1980). *Culture's consequences: International differences in work-related values.* Beverly Hills, CA: Sage.

15. House, R.J., Javidan, M., Dorfman, P.W. & de Luque, M.S. (2006). A failure of scholarship: Response to George Graen's critique of GLOBE. *Academy of Management Perspectives*, 102-114.

16. Chhokar, J.S., Brodbeck, F.C. & House, R.J. (2007). Introduction. In J. S. Chhokar, F. C. Brodbeck, & R. J. House (Eds.), *Culture and leadership across the world: The GLOBE book of in-depth studies of 25 societies* (pp. xiii-xvi). Mahwah, NJ: Lawrence Erlbaum Associates.

17. Brodbeck, F.C., Chhokar, J.S. and House, R.J. (2007). Culture and leadership in 25 societies: Integration, conclusions, and future directions. In J. S. Chhokar, F. C. Brodbeck, & R. J. House (Eds.), *Culture and leadership across the world: The GLOBE book of in-depth studies of 25 societies* (pp. 1023-1084). Mahwah, NJ: Lawrence Erlbaum Associates.

Hofstede, G. (2006). What did GLOBE really measure? Researchers' minds versus respondents' minds? *Journal of International Business Studies*, 37, 882-896.

Graen, G.B. (2006). In the eye of the beholder: Cross-cultural lesson in leadership from Project GLOBE: A response viewed from the third culture bonding (TCB) model of cross-cultural leadership. *Academy of Management Perspectives*, 20(4), 95- 101.

18. Douglas, M. (1978). *Cultural Bias*, London: Royal Anthropological Institute

Thompson, M., Ellis, R. & Wildavsky, A. (1990). *Cultural Theory*, Westview Press, Colorado, CO

19. Triandis, H.C. (1994). *Culture and Social Behavior.* New York, NY: McGraw-Hill.

20. Hall, Edward T. (1976). *Beyond Culture.* Garden City, NY: Doubleday Anchor Books.

21. Triandis, H.C. (2000). Culture and conflict. *International Journal of Psychology*, 35(2), 145-152

22. De Cieri, H., Dowling, P.J. & Taylor, K.F. (1991). The psychological impact of expatriate relocation on partners. *The International Journal of Human Resource Management*, 2(3), 377-414.

23. Manev, I.M. & Stevenson, W.B. (2001). Nationality, cultural distance, and expatriate status: Effects on the managerial network in a multinational enterprise. *Journal of International Business Studies*, 32(2), 285-303.

24. Valentine, D. (2001). Intercultural business communication, international students, and experiential learning. *Business Communication Quarterly*, 64(4), 90-104.

25. Kogut, B. & Singh, H. (1988). The effect of National Culture on the choice of Entry Mode. *Journal of International Business Studies*, 19(3): 411-432

26. Chang, S.J. (1995). International Expansion Strategy of Japanese Firms: Capability Building through Sequential Entry. *Academy of Management Journal.* 38, 383-407

27. Li, J.T. & Guisinger S. (1991). Comparative Business Failures of Foreign Controlled Firms in United States. *Journal of International Business Studies*, 22(2): 209-224

28. Barkema, H., Shenkar, O., Vermeulen, F. and Bell, J.H. (1997). Working Abroad, Working with others: How firms learn to operate International Joint Ventures. *Academy of Management Journal*, 40, 2, 426-442.

29. Johnson J.L., Cullen J.B. & Sakano T. (1991). *Cultural congruency in international joint ventures.* Proceedings of Eastern Academy of Management International Conference, Nice, *France*.

30. Park, S.H. & Ungson G.R. (1997). The effect of National Culture. Organizational Complimentarity and Economic Motivation on Joint Venture Dissolution. *Academy of Management Journal*, 40, 2, 279-307.

31. Rathje, S. (2007). Intercultural Competence: The Status and Future of a Controversial Concept. *Journal for Language and Intercultural Communication*, 7(4), p.254–266

32. Osland, JS, Bird, A. (2000). Beyond sophisticated stereotyping: Cultural sense making in context. *Academy of Management Executive*, Vol. 14 Issue 1, p65

33. Madison, Greg (2006). "Existential Migration", *Existential Analysis* 17 (2): 238–60.

34. Witte, A. (2012). "Making the Case for a Post-National Cultural Analysis of Organizations," *Journal of Management Inquiry*, 21:141. Originally published online on 13 September 2011.

35. Holden, Nigel (2001). *Cross-cultural Management: A Knowledge Management Perspective*, Financial Times Management

Online resources for this chapter, available at:
http://www.vijeshjain.com/books/multinational-workplaces/resources/chapter-3

4. IMPACT OF SOCIETAL CULTURES ON ORGANIZATIONS

Who are we here? Well, how about there? What about elsewhere? Today's global organizations are facing these questions as they try to determine their organizational identity[1] across many different work locations across the world. Understanding diverse cultural perspectives has become critical[2] not only for the purpose of recruitment and retention, but also for maximizing employees' contributions to and identification of themselves with the organization they work for. Researches to explore the phenomenon of how societal culture influences organizational identity in a global organization, has been done in the past[3]. For example, focus of one of these researches had been on "how the local societal cultures, in which regional offices of multinational enterprises are located – as defined by the nine cultural dimensions for the GLOBE (Global Leadership and Organizational Behavior Effectiveness) study[4] – may influence the way the employees of a global organization perceive their organizational identity?" These researches predominantly concluded that besides the dynamics of an integrated and global economy, there are other factors that add to the complexities of hiring and retaining diverse workforce across the globe. For example, a significant factor is 'widespread immigration', which has increased dramatically in the past, especially during past century.

Brodbeck, Chhokar, & House (2007)[5] predicted that instead of converging into an 'amalgam of global cultural standards,' societal cultural differences may become more distinct as people strive 'to preserve their local cultural heritage and social identity'. It appears that the global locations of organizations, coupled with the growing cultural diversity of the workforce, have created significant challenges for organizations. A better understanding is needed of how employees from multi societal cultures with different values and cultural practices perceives the identity of the organization, they work for, as well as how understanding those perceptions can foster more effective identification with the organization.

Societal cultures, commemoration and identity

The influence of societal cultures in the process and outcomes of commemoration and their link to identity has been studied extensively in sociology[6]. Factors that influence commemoration include shared values, emotions, language[7], and generations[8]. Commemoration is consistently connected with identity at both the individual and collective levels in that the 'construction of a person's identity as a member of a group not only implies coherence with the past but also with the other individuals sharing that past' [9]. As *Frijda* (1997)[9] noted the shared identity may extend to a small group such as a family or larger groups such as societies or nations. Researchers who focus on national cultures suggest that cultural memories affirm a nation's identity[10]. *Hodgkin and Radstone* (2003)[11] proposed that 'nationalist memory describes the geography of belonging, an identity forged in a specified landscape inseparable from it'.

Schwartz and Kim (2002)[12] found that recollection of critical events is patterned in accordance with the specific cultural themes that comprise a national identity scheme. In their study, for example, the *US*, identity scheme emphasized independence, quality, individualized, populism, feelings of triumph, and dominance as compared to the *Korean* identity schema, which emphasized interdependence, hierarchy, and honor. Other researchers took a broader perspective and suggested that the commemoration process is linked primarily to shared values and interaction that may extend beyond national boundaries in that the 'past constitutes a resource for creating community among those with shared values and common interests who are embedded in networks of interaction' [13].

Cultural identity, cultural diversity and group dynamics

Cultural identity may have a major impact on group dynamics in international project teams for their success. Understanding certain elements of a culture which represent a true measure of cultural identity and its impact on group dynamics may be a difficult task. However, there are several aspects of cultural identity which may be analyzed with common knowledge. A quote from 'The Art of Travel' by *Bottom, A.D.* (2004)[14]

illustrates well the complexity of cultural identity (see exhibit 4.1)

Exhibit 4.1

"Ever since he was a boy *Flaubert* had the habit of denying he was a Frenchman. He deeply detested his home country, France and fellow his countrymen. He had a lifelong yearning for being an Egyptian. He proposed a new perspective for determining a person's nationality. He suggested that nationality should not be based on the place you are born or the family you come from, but on one's longing for particular places.

It was later for *Flaubert* to stretch this theory of development of identity to 'gender' and 'species', so that at one time he declared that in essence he was a camel, a bear and a woman. 'I feel like buying a painting of a bear, having it framed, hanging it in my bedroom and calling it 'Portrait of *Gustave Flaubert*' in order to represent my moral conditions and behavior patterns'.

An understanding of cultural identity, coupled with management styles and leadership styles which work in diverse cultures can improve a large proportion of cross cultural awareness which is urgently required in international project teams. In its normal course, such understanding may take a long time to trickle into the real life work places. As CEO of Unilever, *Antony Burgmans*, states in an interview with the *Dutch* newspaper NRC *Handelsblad*: "it took us most of the last century to create the cross-cultural awareness that we now have in the management structure."Therefore an understanding of cultural identity and its impact on group dynamics is important.

However, more important is the debate whether national cultures may have an impact on individual behavior in group dynamics or is it that individual personalities, likes and dislikes irrespective of their national origin, defines the so called cultural diversity in cross cultural teams working on international projects. Classic authors on cross-cultural aspects of leadership, such as *Hall* (1966)[15], *Hofstede* (1980)[16] and *Trompenaars* (1997)[17] have emphasized the importance of understanding cross-cultural differences within international teams and they all conclude national cultures may have a significant impact on individual behavior in group dynamics. *Schneider* and *Barsoux* (2002)[18] say "there is a strong impact of national culture on effective management and of utilizing differences to create competitive advantage for multinational firms".

There are others who emphasize that many of the differences that team members bring to a team are rooted in their personality structure or professional identity and not in their cultural background. *Laurent, A.* (1997)[19] provides an example of professional identity overriding the impact of national culture of his research into *French* and *German* multinational corporations. He looked at finance professionals from *France* and *Germany*, working for the same corporation, and found them to be more similar in their way than a sample of *French* finance and *French* marketing professionals. Others like *Miller* (1993)[20] and *Katzenbach* (1994)[21] emphasize that a team is a group of individuals working for a common purpose, and the secret of building a strong team is to infuse a clear common purpose and ensuring the identification by each member with a common group task.

Cultural identities themselves may be the combination of core identity and certain partial identities. These partial identities may include professional identity, gender, sexual orientation, social class and educational background. Cultural core identities may be a web of complex combination of individual personalities which may differ based on their origin and family background as also several environmental factors of the societies they live in or belong to. These aspects may also include certain types of stereotypes, biases, religious beliefs, ease of understanding others, views about the world around them, historical factors and several other stimuli. This perspective takes us to an interesting set of comfort variables for inquiry into the composition and structure of a workable model of CFC.

Impact on organizations

The theory and research on the intersection of societal cultures, national cultures and organizational cultures have been drawn primarily from *Hofstede's* (1980, 1992)[22] work that asserts that cultural differences between nations can be described and measured in a set of dimensions that reflect answers to 'universal problems of human societies' [23]. More recently, others have suggested a homogenization[24] or convergence view[25] of globalization, where national cultural differences are 'being replaced by global corporate cultures and universal organizational identification' [26]. A third perspective would agree that countries and societies play a major role in the construction of social reality in global organizations. Yet within a national culture[27,] multiple social identities may exist. Researchers have investigated differentiation and plurality among employees as well as the consumers within a specific country or society[26].

McSweeney (2002)[28] and others have challenged the intra nation homogeneity assumption in *Hofstede's* work, suggesting that it does not take into account the agency of individuals in defining and shaping this identity[27], and related researches have focused on the complexity of these relationships. A study by *Jack* and *Lorbiecki's* (2007)[26] has emphasized the role of national identity in organizational identification and at the same time has also contradicted the received wisdom in the cross-cultural management (CCM) literature which attributes a certain amount of homogeneity to the concept of national identity. It introduced further complexity to this relationship by asserting that organizational identity should be thought of as differentially constructed according to the complex interdependencies of the level of identity in question, the nature of dominant discourses with an organization and the social and cultural position of the individual[26].

Conclusion

The chapter discussed the theoretical foundations and growing incidences of the phenomenon of deferring identification of employees of an organization with it based on their differing cultural background. It also discussed different perspective towards the impact of societal cultures in organizations and the significance of cultural identity in driving employee behavior in MNEs to desired goals and success. The chapter has also argued differing perspectives of different researchers on the impact on the national identity in defining organizational identification. In between the chapter has also argued that national identity may have an impact on the team performance in a multicultural environment at multinational workplaces. It also forms one of the major reasons why an understanding of different cultural perspectives and their relation to the organizational identity, is becoming very important for strategic management of multinational firms.

Suggested questions for discussion:

1) Why has strategic importance of understanding different cultural perspectives, increased for MNEs in current times? Discuss with examples.
2) Do you think in a globalized world of today, there are local forces which try to retain their social heritage and local identities? Discuss with examples.
3) If growing cultural diversity of the work force, coupled with global locations of the several offices and operations, creates immense challenges for today's multinational corporations, why do these organizations do not mind going places across the world and tend to employ multicultural work force? Discuss
4) Do you think societal cultures with differences in values and cultural practices perceive the identity of the organizations, they work for, differently? Discuss
5) What could be the role of commemoration as a link between

societal cultures and organizational identity? How are these terms connected to each other? Explain with examples.

6) What impact cultural identity and cultural diversity have on the team dynamics at multicultural workplaces? Discuss.

Notes:

1. Albert, S. & Whetten, D.A. (1985). Organizational Identity. In LL Cummings & BM Staw (Eds.) *Research in organizational behavior.* Vol.7: 263-295, Greenwich. CT: JAI Press.

2. House, R., Javidan, M. & Dorfman, P. W. (2001). *Project GLOBE: An introduction. Applied Psychology: An International Review*, 50(4), 489-505.

3. Ekmekci, Ozgur, (2009). The Role of Frontline Employees in Building Sustainable Customer Service, *SAM Advanced Management Journal*, Vol. 74.2009, 4, p. 11-21

4. House, R.J., Javidan, M., Dorfman, P.W. & de Luque, M.S. (2006). A failure of scholarship: Response to George Graen's critique of GLOBE. *Academy of Management Perspectives*, 102-114.

5. Brodbeck, F.C., Chhokar, J.S. and House, R.J. (2007). Culture and leadership in 25 societies: Integration, conclusions, and future directions. In J. S. Chhokar, F. C. Brodbeck, & R. J. House (Eds.), *Culture and leadership across the world: The GLOBE book of in-depth studies of 25 societies* (pp. 1023-1084). Mahwah, NJ: Lawrence Erlbaum Associates.

6. Hodgkin, K., & Radstone, S. (Eds.) (2003). Introduction. In Contested pasts. *The politics of memory* (pp. 1-21). London: Routledge.

    Schwartz, B. & Kim, M. (2002). Honor, dignity and collective memory. In K. Cerulo (Ed.), *Culture in mind* (pp. 209-226). London: Routledge.

7. Pennebaker, J.W. & Banasik, B.L. (1997). *On the creation and maintenance of collective memories: History of social psychology.* In J. W. Pennebaker, D. Paez & B. Rime (Eds.), *Collective memory of political events.* Social psychological perspectives (pp. 3-19). Mahwah, NJ: Lawrence Erlbaum Associates.

8. Schuman, H., Belli, R.F. & Bischoping, K. (1997). *The generational bias of historical knowledge.* In J. W. Pennebaker, D. Paez, & B. Rime (Eds.), Collective memory of political events. Mahwah, NJ: Lawrence Erlbaum Associates.

9. Frijda, N.H. (1997). *Commemorating.* In J. W. Pennebaker, D. Paez, & B. Rime (Eds.), Collective memory of political events. Social psychological

perspectives (pp. 103-127). Mahwah, NJ: Lawrence Erlbaum Associates.

10. Carr, W. (2003). Germany's Black Holocaust, 1890-1945: The Untold Truth! Paperback, Scholar Technological Institute of Research, Inc. (June 2003)

11. Hodgkin, K., & Radstone, S. (Eds.) (2003). *Introduction. In Contested pasts.* The politics of memory (pp. 1-21). London: Routledge.

12. Schwartz, B. & Kim, M. (2002). Honor, dignity and collective memory. In K. Cerulo (Ed.), *Culture in mind* (pp. 209-226). London: Routledge.

13. Fine, G. (2007). *The construction of historical equivalence: Weighing the red and the brown scares.* Symbolic Interaction, 30(1), 27-39.

14. Bottom, A.D. (2004). *The Art of Travel,* Hamish Hamilton, London

15. Hall, E. (1966). *The Hidden Dimension,* Anchor Books, Doubleday

16. Hofstede, G. (1980). *Culture's consequences: International differences in work-related values.* Beverly Hills, CA: Sage.

17. Trompenaars F. & Hampden-Turner, C. (1997). *Riding the waves of culture: Understanding diversity in global business* (2nd Ed.). New York: McGraw-Hill.

18. Schneider & Barsoux (2002). Managing across cultures, *Financial Times,* Prentice Hall

19. Laurent, A. (1997). Reinventer l'art du management au Carrefour des cultures, *7th Sietar Europa Annual Congress – book of proceedings*

20. Miller, E. (1993). *From dependency to autonomy; studies in organization and change,* FAB London

21. Katzenbach & Smith (1994). *The wisdom of teams,* Harper Business

22. Hofstede, G. (1980). *Culture's consequences: International differences in work-related values.* Beverly Hills, CA: Sage.

    Hofstede, G. (1992). *Cultures and organizations: Software of the mind.* New York McGraw-Hill.

23. Hofstede, G. (2006). What did GLOBE really measure? Researchers' minds versus respondents' minds? *Journal of International Business Studies,* 37, 882-896.

24. Howes, D. (1996). *Cross-cultural consumption: Global markets, local realities.* London: Routledge.

25. Dorfman, P.W., Hanges, P.J. & Brodbeck, F.C. (2004). *Leadership and*

cultural variation: The identification of culturally endorsed leadership profiles. In R. J. House, P. J. Hanges, M. Javidan, P. W. Dorfman, & V. Gupta (Eds.), Culture, leadership and organizations. The GLOBE study of 62 societies (pp. 669-720). Thousand Oaks, CA: Sage Publications.

26. Jack, G. & Lorbiecki, A. (2007). National identity, globalization and the discursive construction of organizational identity - *British Journal of Management*, 18, S79-94

27. Ailon-Souday, G. & Kunda, G. (2003). The local selves of global workers: The social construction of national identity in the face of organizational globalization. Organization Studies, 23(7), 1073-1096.

28. McSweeney, Brendan (2002). *Hofstede's* Model of National Cultural Differences and Their Consequences: A Triumph of Faith - A Failure of Analysis. *Human Relations* 55 (1)

Online resources for this chapter, available at:
http://www.vijeshjain.com/books/multinational-workplaces/resources/chapter-4

5. RESEARCH RELATED TO CFC

While the phenomenon of CFC has not been given due attention till date, by social scientists, especially in the context of impact on organizations, following discussion on two very important research studies gives great insights into the way the CFC at multinational workplaces can be investigated. First study relates to the global view of generation Y involving a five country research conducted on students of different universities in these five countries. Most importantly variables studied in these studies give a strong guidance about how any 'factors based' investigations are to be carried out for understanding the phenomenon of CFC. Similarly, second research on 'interaction comfort' conducted on students of US universities and coming from diverse cultural background, gives important insights into the concept of CFC, although this research study is limited in its scope to the context of 'service quality'.

Global view of generation Y

A worldview refers to the possessing of an attitude that positively embraces sensitivity to and acceptance of cultural differences. *Lassk* (2004)[1] compared the worldview of a sample of members from 'generation Y' (born between 1975 and 1995) from five nations and analyzed them in relation to what would be expected as a result of their 'world view' by applying *Hofstede's* typology of cultural orientations and the real 'world view' of them. While 'generation Y' often is used to describe as a US demographic phenomenon, many of the basic characteristics of this group go beyond national borders. In particular, this group has been found to be heavily influenced by the availability of information and learning from a wide variety of modern and traditional media. This group has also grown up with things like 'computers', 'fast food culture', 'pop music', '*Tiananmen* square' and the 'Internet' among others. They are more independent, cynical and demanding than their previous generations.

The 'worldview' concept implies an inclusive approach to cultural appreciation; one that neutralizes the tendency to embrace and uphold one's native culture at the expense of others. Five factors were studied in this study, to understand this world view-

1. Trust of foreigners,

2. Interest in learning foreign languages,

3. Interest to live abroad

4. Interest in meeting with foreigners and

5. Belief in the concept of global Village/common global cultures.

The study hypothesized that out of the five countries studied, namely – *USA*, *China*, *Egypt*, *Belgium* and *Mexico*, countries which are weak in 'uncertainty avoidance' than others are likely to indicate

a) More willingness to live abroad,

b) More interested to meet foreigners,

c) Having more trust for foreigners, and

d) More interested in learning foreign languages.

Similarly, countries which are more individualistic are less likely to hold the belief in the concept of the global village and that most cultures have things in common. A third hypothesis of the study postulated that countries which are having smaller 'power distance' are likely to be more comfortable and having more trust in foreigners and more interested in meeting foreigners than others.

The findings of the study indicated that '*USA* sample' (weak 'uncertainty') is more willing than other countries to live abroad. On the other hand, '*Mexico* sample' (high 'uncertainty') was the least willing to live abroad. This was in line with the hypothesis as postulated on the basis of *Hofstede's* typology. However, China sample (weak 'uncertainty') is found to be less willing to live abroad nullifying the hypothesis and also the applicability of the *Hofstede's* typology on this worldview dimension. Another hypothesis also proposed that '*USA* and *China* samples' (among weak 'uncertainty' cultures) were more likely to be more interested in meeting other persons from foreign countries. However, empirical results showed that the opposite is true for '*Chinese* sample'.

It was also proposed that national cultures that are weak in 'uncertainty avoidance' are likely to be more comfortable with foreigners and more interested in learning a foreign language than samples that are strong on uncertainty avoidance. No support is found for either of these hypotheses. Only partial support was found for the hypothesis that small 'power distance' countries like *USA* is more likely to be comfortable with foreigners and more willing to meet with foreigners. *USA* sample was not really more interested in meeting with foreigners than large 'power distance countries'. Two of the three 'collectivist countries' samples (*China* and *Mexico*), but not the *Egypt* sample, believed more strongly than the Individualistic countries (*USA* and *Belgium* samples) that most cultures have things in common.

In short, in this empirical test of *Hofstede's* typology, results suggested that three dimensions - 'uncertainty avoidance', 'individualism', and 'power distance'; and the managerial implications associated with each of these dimensions; do not hold very well for generation Y's worldview. In other words, *Hofstede's* typology is not a strong predictor of generation Y's worldview according to this research study. Therefore, existing knowledge of the world cultures and its cultural dimensions may not explain the pattern of the 'worldview' of the future managers.

Since, a 'worldview' signifies possessing of an attitude which positively embraces the sensitivity to and acceptance of cultural differences, the research has several clues to the phenomenon of CFC at international, multicultural workplaces in MNEs. It is easy to imply that *Hofstede's* typology is not really a strong predictor of the phenomenon of CFC, indicating the concept need to be studied independently and also indicating CFC may also denote an independent cultural dimension for studying cultural differences across nations. Although it provides a view to hold for multicultural team managers, a starting point to an effective cross cultural management at MNE workplaces, more work was needed to study the concept of CFC and its group dynamics.

Cross cultural 'interaction comfort'

Other notable research related to 'level of CFC' is 'cross-cultural interaction comfort and service evaluation' [2]. The study empirically tested the notion of respondent's being comfortable during social interactions in a foreign country (interaction comfort) and its impact on 'how service quality is evaluated by the respondent'. The results showed that the 'home country social class' of the respondents is positively associated with 'interaction comfort'. In addition, similarities or dissimilarities between one's home and one's host country environment during respondent's overseas travels also influenced this cross cultural 'interaction comfort'.

Surprisingly the length of stay in the host country, even when the visitors have an opportunity to interact with local people, did not have a strong impact on the cross cultural 'interaction comfort'. It means irrespective of the opportunity of the traveler to acquire a certain comfort level after a certain period of stay in the host country, the comfort level does not seem to improve. The results also indicated that visitors already high on 'interaction comfort' in conducive situation in the host country were more satisfied with the services offered in the host country and were willing to advocate it to others back home. These research implications gave useful directions to the subject of this book.

This study was subjected to the international students in *US* universities for a variety of educational courses. However the study did not take into account the services directly related to the 'exchange of education' which was the core services availed, rather it studied the service delivery of the augmented services, like housing, financial issues, campus safety, loneliness, etc. Study primarily based its theoretical context on theories related to dichotomy of high context and low context cultures, cultural distance, language differences, ethnic commonality etc.

Conclusion

The two research discussed in this chapter clearly show that there is a strong case to identify the variables which are likely to influence the cultural differences explaining the phenomenon of CFC. The inferences drawn from these researches also show that these levels are likely to vary from country to country and existing cultural models may not be able to predict such cultural differences especially in the organizational context. These studies also provide important clues to certain observed and latent variables which may play an important part in understanding the dynamics of 'level of CFC' at multinational workplaces.

Suggested questions for discussion:

1) How do differences in the worldview of managers at multicultural workplaces are likely to impact their contribution to the success or failure of the organization they work for? Discuss

2) Do you think differences in cultural background based on the country of origin of employees are likely to result in differences in

the world view of the team members of a multicultural team? Discuss

3) Discuss the implications of differing 'interaction comfort' of travelers on their evaluation of service quality in a host country?

Notes:

1. Lassk & Fugate, (2004). *A Cross-Cultural Comparison of Future Managers' Worldviews: Does Hofstede's Typology Apply To Generation Y?*

2. Paswan, A.K. et al., (2005). Cross-cultural Interaction Comfort and Service Evaluation. *Journal of International Consumer Marketing*, 18(1/2)

Online resources for this chapter, available at:
http:/www.vijeshjain.com/books/multinational-workplaces/resources/chapter-5

6. CULTURAL VARIABLES OF CFC

When persons with a distant cultural origin, is exposed to an alien culture in a host country, it may be difficult to feel comfortable until he or she is able to appreciate the new environment. This discomfort behavior may manifest in peculiar behavior which can result into friction, conflict or a complaining behavior. For example international students coming to study in the US, may show diverse reactions to new environment depending upon their own seasoning of mind which they carry due to their own cultural origin. Students from *Asian* countries like *Korea, China, and Taiwan* are likely to show a different kind of discomfort than, for example students coming from *the West or East European countries*. Clearly possibility of the second set of students being more comfortable in a new environment is much more than the first set. At multicultural workplaces a similar phenomenon may be observable due to cultural differences among team members.

Language proficiency may also play an important role initially in such cases. But more clearly core cultural components like - cultural stereotypes, biases and discrimination[1], preferred leadership styles in different cultures[2], patriotic feelings (world value survey), values, ethics and beliefs[3,4,5] and demographic factors will have major play. These variables have interaction with other inherent variables (uncontrollable variables) coming from outside influences (natural or man-made) and from the origins of the specific cultures. In simple terms, this comfort dynamics seem to be the result of a complex mix of several cultural elements. These elements may differ substantially among distant cultures. The nature of some of these variables is discussed in more details in the following paragraphs.

Stereotypes, prejudice and discrimination

Stereotypes, prejudice and discrimination are understood to be related to each other but are different concepts[6]. Stereotypes are regarded as the most cognitive component, prejudice as the affective and discrimination as the behavioral component of prejudicial reactions[7]. In this triangular view of intergroup behavior, stereotypes reflect expectations and beliefs about the characteristics of members of groups perceived as 'culturally different' from one's own, prejudice represents the emotional response to certain cues and triggers initiated by 'culturally different' persons in the cross cultural teams, and discrimination refers to the actions most likely by the local members of the group[7]. Although related to each other, this tri polar view can co-exist independently of each other[8]. According to *Katz, D. and Braly K.* (1935)[9], stereotyping leads to racial prejudice when people emotionally react to the name of a group, ascribe characteristics to members of that group, and then evaluate those characteristics.

Possible prejudicial effects of stereotypes are[10]-

1. Justification of ill-founded prejudices or ignorance or views;
2. Not giving a chance to rethink one's attitudes and behavior towards a group, which may be a victim of such stereotypical behavior;
3. Preventing some people of stereotyped groups from acting or succeeding in activities or different fields[11].

Self-stereotyping

Stereotypes can impact self-evaluations and lead to something called - self-stereotyping[12,10]. For instance, *Correll* (2001, 2004)[13] found that common stereotypes (e.g., the stereotype that women have weaker mathematical ability) affect women's and men's correct evaluations of their abilities (e.g., in math and science), such that men think of their own ability to do a task higher than that of women, performing at the same level. Similarly, a study by *Sinclair* et al. (2006)[12] has shown that when their stereotype that *'Asian Americans* excel in math' was highlighted, *Asian American* women rated their math ability more favorably. In contrast, they rated their math ability less favorably when their gender and the corresponding stereotype of women's inferior math skills were highlighted. *Sinclair* et al. (2006)[12] found, a relationship with the endorsement of the stereotypes by close people in someone's life. Therefore people's self-stereotyping can increase or decrease depending on whether close others endorse or oppose those stereotypes.

Ethnocentrism and prejudice

Although the world is not yet a 'global village' that *Ted Levitt* (1985)[14] predicted, an increasing number of consumer markets in different parts of the world are characterized by global competition. A growing number of companies in many industries now operate on a global level. However, most of the regionally focused companies selling regional culture specific products are not operating globally due to lack of consumers of culturally different products in many parts of the world. This is also true on a national level. For example, companies operating in *Indian* southern states, focusing on traditional south *India* clothing may not be operating from north or with the same set of products. It shows that consumer behavior for culturally different products may be still averse. This behavior may be the result of several factors.

The trend towards globalization of markets of culturally different and foreign products can be fueled by changes in consumer knowledge and behavior. Satellite television and frequent travel overseas have made consumers more aware of other cultures' lifestyles and products, and increased the possibility of international brands to become national. While some consumers may prefer culturally different products and view them as symbols of uniqueness, others exhibit strong preferences for locally-made culturally adapted products and may have negative attitudes towards culturally different or foreign products and services. Such negative attitudes towards culturally different and foreign products can arise from a number of sources. Consumers may think products from certain countries are inferior quality, hold feelings of prejudice toward a particular region[15], or may even consider it wrong, almost immoral, to buy culturally different and foreign products[16].

Previous research on consumer attitudes towards culturally different or foreign goods and services have typically focused on the impact of a single factor such as consumer ethnocentric attitudes. However, other research[15] suggests that the influences, describing the tendency to buy culturally different and foreign product may be considerably more complex, resulting from the interaction of various different factors. These factors may include prejudice, ethnocentrism, superstitions, lack of awareness, etc. In all, tendency to buy culturally different or foreign products may indicate level of comfort of local cultures with culturally different and foreign cultures.

Willingness to explore distant or foreign cultures

Why do people want to explore the unknown? Why people get curious to know the unknown? Are curiosity and exploration motivations or drives?

Are curiosity and exploration, independent of one another? Do different cultures have different propensity to explore the unknown or distant cultures? Researches in these areas are still not conclusive.

'Motivation' is defined as the arousal, direction and persistence of behavior[17]; an internal condition that activates behavior and gives it direction to carry out an activity. The drive is defined as a basic or instinctive need to accomplish a task. On the other hand curiosity is defined as a need, thirst or desire for knowledge. However the concept of 'curiosity' is prime to 'motivation'. *Berlyne* (1960)[18] believes that curiosity is a motivational prerequisite for 'exploratory tendencies' in humans. 'Exploration' refers to all activities concerned with gathering information about the alien environment or unknown. *Langevin* (1971)[19] has conducted research in the area of 'curiosity' and classified measures of curiosity into two categories. First, curiosity is viewed as a 'motivational state' and measured by behavioral indices. Second, he conceptualized curiosity as a 'personality trait' that is assessed by 'personality measures'. For *Fowler* (1965)[20], 'boredom' is one 'prerequisite or motivation' for curiosity or exploration.

There is evidence for similarities in cross-cultural behavior in the context of exploration[21]. However, cultures generally are different in terms of attitudes towards exploration and information seeking. This is especially true for the sensation-seeking motive. *Zuckerman* (1994)[22] defines sensation seeking as 'the aspiration for varied, novel, complex and intense sensations and experiences, and still having the willingness to take physical, social, legal, and financial risks for the sake of such experiences.' *Berlyne* (1960)[18] also conducted studies on cross cultural comparisons in the area of curiosity and exploration. His findings concluded that there is a high level of similarity between 'demand characteristics' of 'stimuli' in the two cultures of widely differing historical antecedents and technological development. Also, different cultures from various geographical regions show evidence for cross-cultural similarities in exploratory behavior.

However, these researches are all inconclusive. It has been reported that more research is needed to study, curiosity behavior in its own cultural context to gain a better understanding of the functional relationships between various environmental and social facilitators and inhibitors of curiosity in a given society.

Views about globalization

Cultural homogenization is an aspect of cultural globalization[23] listed as one of its main characteristics[24], and may even refer to the reduction in cultural diversity[25] through the popularization and diffusion of a wide array of cultural cues both physical objects and non physical ones as customs, ideas and values[24]. *O'Connor* (2006)[26] defines it as 'the process by which local cultures are transformed or absorbed by a dominant outside culture.' 'Cultural homogenization' has been ranked as 'perhaps the most widely discussed hallmark of global culture' [24]. Cultural homogenization in theory could lead to the development of a single global culture and elimination of all other, local cultures included[24]. Cultural homogenization or globalization can impact national or regional identities and culture, which would be 'eroded by the impact of global or national cultural industries and multinational or national media[27].

However, while some scholars are critical of this process, others note that the process of cultural homogenization is not one-way, and in fact involves a number of cultures exchanging various elements[24, 25]. They explain that as a different cultures mix, homogenization is less about the spread of a single culture as about the mixture of different cultures, as people become aware of other cultures and adopt their elements[24, 25, 28, 29]. Examples of such phenomenon can be derived from things like - *non-western* culture affecting the *West* includes world music and the popularization of *non-western* television (*Latin American telenovelas*, Japanese anime, *Indian Bollywood*), religion (*Islam, Buddhism*), food, and clothing in the *West*[25, 29,30]. Different cultures may have different views about cultural homogenization. There are certain cultures which see advantages in cultural homogenization viewing the process as intermixing of more than one culture and no domination of a single culture. There are others which are more critical of the process. Such differences of views may indicate the differences in terms of CFC.

The above researches form the basis of current research into the enquiry into the understanding of intercultural comfort dynamics of 'multi cultural international project teams'.

Values and beliefs

Although there had been no evidence of any past research about the direct impact of values differences in level of CFC, there is definitely an impact of value differences on the team results[3,4]. (See table 6.1)

Table 6.1: Differences of values between western cultures and non-western cultures

Western Cultural Values	Non-Western Cultural Values	Impact on Team Performance
Guilt (self-control)	Shame (ext. control)	None
Achievement	Modesty	None
Equality or Egalitarianism	Hierarchy (several cases)	–ive

Winning	Collaboration/Harmony	+ive
Time is money	Time equivalent to life	–ive
Self Pride	Saving of face	None
Respect for competence	Respect for elders	–ive
Tasks	Relationship/Loyalty	–ive
Action/Doing	Being/Acceptance	–ive
Control	Fate	–ive
Informal Behavior	Formal Behavior	–ive
Directness/Assertiveness	Indirectness	–ive
Future	Past	–ive
Ready for change	Stick to traditions	–ive
Respect to results	Respect for status/Ascription	+ive
Individualism	Collectivism/Group	+ive
Specific/Linear	Holistic	+ive
Verbal Communication	Nonverbal communication	+ive

Source: Marquardt and Kearsley (1999)[3]; Kohls (1981)[4]

Table 6.1 above lists 'values differences' between western and non-western cultures and how these differences may have an impact on international projects and working on the 'cross cultural teams'. In this table, (+ive) indicates positive impact of combining both values on outcomes, while (-ive) indicate a negative impact of combining both values on outcomes (culture clash). On the same note (None) indicate no direct impact on outcomes.

Impact of cultural factors on level of CFC

Taking cue from above discussions, the authors of this book proposed a theoretical scheme to understand the basis which explains the observed controllable and uncontrollable factors which lead to a level of comfort of local cultures with foreign cultures (See figure 6.1).

These elements may differ substantially among distant cultures. As per this proposition, although we have an idea of possible latent variables which comprise of the consequent level of CFC, we still need to test the model to identify exact latent variables (or CFC variables) which explain the concept of CFC. Among the main objectives of this book is to find these latent variables which form the actual composition of 'level of CFC'. These variables can provide useful information into the nature of the latent behavior of local cultures vis-a-vis foreign cultures to provide a framework for CFC at multicultural workplaces.

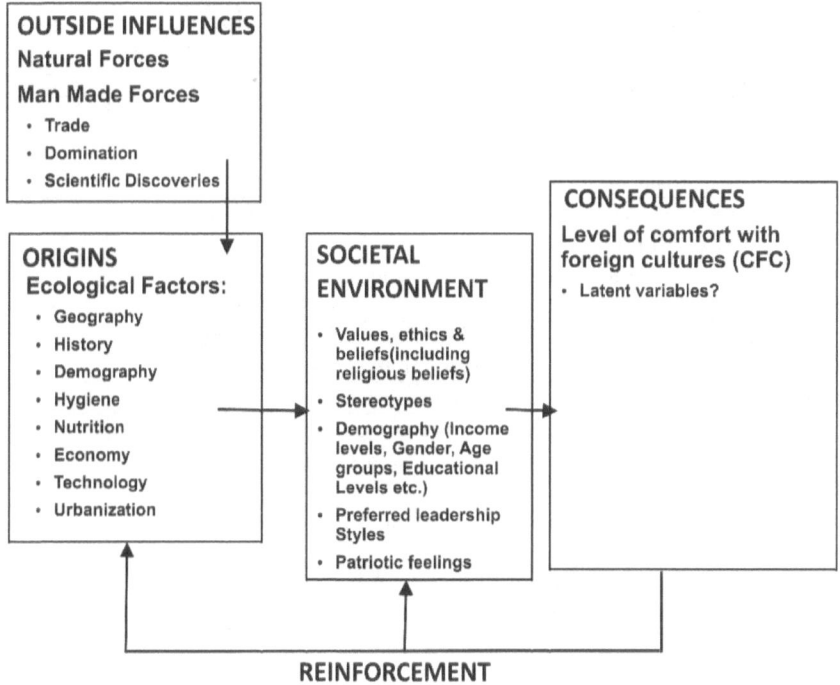

Figure 6.1: Observed variables for level of CFC.
(*Source*: Based on *Hofstede*, 2001, p12)[32]

Identification of observed cultural variables

Based on several other arguments and using a series of brainstorming sessions, the authors arrived at a list of directly observable elements which can form the basis of empirical studies on the dynamics of intercultural comfort at multinational workplaces. These observed variables were categorized for two kinds of empirical treatments for further investigation into the CFC modeling. One was to use the variables in an empirical study based on secondary data and the other was to carry out a primary empirical study using a survey instrument. The 2 sets of observed variables are given in tables 6.2 and 6.3.

It may be noted that for the purpose of estimating the CFC scores for different national cultures certain weights were given to each of these observed variables in the case of the first set so that a secondary data investigation is possible. These weights were based on a multistage *Delphi* method of 'perception scaling and consultative process' involving around 200 cross cultural experts and students.

Table 6.2: Final CFC Parameters and Weights Allocation.

Sings	Parameters	Weights
MS	Effect of Multicultural Society: Effect of society not being substantially multicultural	10%
NR	Impact of Native's Response: Adverse response of a common native to a foreigner	20%
BC	Impact of Bureaucracy: unfavorable impact of bureaucratic setup to the comfort of a foreigner	10%
IP	Effect of Immigrant Population: Effect of non existence of substantial immigrant population in the country	5%
RM	Effect of Racism (based on skin color)	15%
GA	Government's Attitude towards Immigrants: Effect of unfavorable attitude of the state towards entry of foreigners (policy making)	10%
RT	Effect of Religious Tolerance: Effect of religious intolerance in the society	15%
EA	Impact of business owner's attitude: Adverse business owner's attitude towards foreign workers or business partners	15%

Table 6.3: CFC questionnaire as a result of focus group discussions and Delphi sessions

---

PART 1 (General observed variables)

Short questions	Full question as used in the questionnaire
Q1: Unrelated person never getting randomly targeted	There are no insecurities related to the sudden turn of events which may result in an unrelated person getting targeted by the society (where I live in) at large
Q2: Problem may not increase with foreigners	The probability of being branded as accused would not increase if the innocent persons also happen to be foreigners
Q3: Rational Society for foreigners	The society (I live in) remains rational in a situation of major crisis involving those which may apparently look like to have been created by certain groups or persons of certain foreign origin or race
Q4: Religious Society	My native society (read country) is religious
Q5: No Victimization of foreigners based on their	I have never witnessed incidents involving a person of foreign origin persecuted or

religious beliefs	victimized for his foreign religious belief in my society
Q6: Curious to know other religious thoughts	I was curious to know more about his/her religious beliefs
Q7: No Global problems due to religious beliefs	I do not think there are problems in the modern world which relates to religious beliefs
Q8: Religion not part of daily life	I do not think religion is a part of my daily life
Q9: No Repulsion with people of other religion	It is not difficult for me to feel close to people who have a different religion from mine
Q10: No existence of a supernatural power	I do not think there exists a supernatural power which may monitor my activities and perhaps influence me in any way
Q11: Belief in the theory of evolution	I believe in the theory of evolution
Q12: No difficulty in understanding of diverse world cultures	I never have any difficulty in understanding of diverse world cultures
Q13: All cultures have the same status	I do not think there are cultures in the world which may be more superior or more refined than others
Q14: No problem to understand foreigners	When dealing with persons of foreign origin I never had difficulty in understanding his or her point of view
Q15: Nothing like my culture represent more values and ethics	I do not think my country's dominant cultures represent more values and ethics than many other cultures of the world
Q16: My culture does not need better recognition	I do not think of the need for my culture getting better recognition in the world of today to solve many of the problems being faced by the humanity
Q17: Learn from other cultures	I always put efforts to learn from other cultures in one way or another
Q18: Fun to learn about foreigners	Getting to know people from another culture is generally fun for me
Q19: Willing to venture into foreign cultures	Not like I may never want to move to a new country, even if I have better prospects mainly due to the fact that I am unwilling to

venture into foreign cultures

Q20: New ideas coming due to globalization	Globalization has resulted in new ideas and positive cultural influences coming into your country from other countries
Q21: No cultural damage by globalization	Globalization of cultures have not damaged my cultural, economic and religious traditions in many ways
Q22: No need to stop globalization	I do not think Something should be done to stop such damage
Q23: Can't stop globalization	Globalization of cultures will happen anyway and cannot be stopped
Q24: Enjoy foreign food	I enjoy eating food of the types originating overseas/from other countries
Q25: Like to visit a foreigner	If I was invited by a foreigner to his house, I will surely follow the invitation
Q26: New learning from visiting a foreigner	If I were invited by a foreigner to visit, it is likely to be a new learning experience for me
Q27: Good feeling to meet a foreigner	I am more likely to feel good to visit a foreigner
Q28: Listen to foreign music	I often listen to foreign music for being different and broadening my world view
Q29: Buy foreign clothing	I like to buy foreign clothing brands because I want to keep up with the global trends in fashion
Q30: Watch foreign movies	I often watch foreign movies because they are windows to different cultures and their ways of life
Q31: Friends must agree with me	I see it's important for me that friends agree with me on most issues
Q32: No problem with a homosexual	I have no issues if someone I know has a homosexual orientation
Q33: No problem with a foreign boss	I would be comfortable with a colleague from a different culture in a superior position to me
Q34: No problem with a foreign junior	I would be comfortable with a colleague from a different culture in an inferior position to me
Q35: No problem with a foreign roommate	I would be comfortable with a roommate from another culture

90

Q36: like to see foreigners coming to my country	I would like seeing people from other countries come to my country
Q37: Comfortable with foreigners	I feel comfortable being around foreigners
Q38: Like to have vacation abroad	If I won a free vacation I would rather spend it in a different country where I am likely to learn about new cultures and ways of life
Q39: Like to know differences to build friendship	Knowing how a person differs from me may help me build our friendship
Q40: Important to learn other cultures	I think it is important to learn more about other cultures
Q41: Cross cultural interaction should be encouraged	Interacting with people from different countries should be encouraged because it will help us improve our own values and beliefs
Q42: Immigrants add value	I consider foreign immigration as a value added our country's economy
Q43: Not like Immigrants getting better salary than us	I d not think Foreigners living and working in our country are being offered better salaries and more respect than our own people
Q44: Immigrants do not steal jobs	I do not think Foreigners living and working in our country are stealing away the benefits and privileges from their rightful owners
Q45: Desire to travel abroad	Not like I have no desire to travel abroad
Q46: I find other cultures are similar to us	If I get to know people from other countries and other cultures, I learn that we are more alike than different
Q47: I will be welcome abroad	Not like I have no desire to travel abroad because I would feel insecure and unwelcome amongst people from a different culture
Q48: Irrational behavior of victims blaming a foreigner	In a situation of certain crisis have you witnessed victims behaving irrationally accusing a certain group of persons based on

their nationality or race?

Q49: Branded accused without proof	Do you think there is a possibility of innocent persons been branded as accused without enough proof in your society
Q50: No encounter with persons preaching their religious beliefs	I have never come across some persons preaching me on his religious orientation

PART 2: (Conditional observed variables)

ST1: Stereotype- Higher Income Group Views

ST1.1: Enterprising Below Income	Below average income persons are generally enterprising enough to look forward to a bright rich future
ST1.2: Below income as Loyal Employees	Below average income persons can generally be trusted as loyal employees
ST1.3: Below income as Trustworthy	Below average income persons can generally be trusted to work given to them for monetary rewards

ST2: Stereotype- Lower Income Group Views

ST2.1: Caring higher income	Above average income persons care about the lower income group
ST2.2: Reliable higher income	Above average income persons can generally be relied on
ST2.3: Helpful higher income	Above average income persons may be willing to help highly needy lower income group persons with money or other resources

ST3: Stereotype-Men's Views

ST3.1: More Chores for women	Women should do more house chores than men
ST3.2: Women more talkative	Women are more talkative and cannot keep an important family secret for long
ST3.3: Women likes to be with women	Women generally like the company of females more than males

ST4: Stereotype- Women's Views

ST4.1: Caring Men	Men generally care enough for the emotions of women
ST4.2: Loving Men	Men generally love the way women want them to be
ST4.3: Respecting Men	Men normally respect women and tend to

give the first right of way

ST5: Stereotype- Situational Discrimination

Have you ever had a problem with a foreigner? If yes answer the following questions

ST5.1: No Problem with countrymen	The problem may not have occurred if the person happened to be a fellow countryman
ST5.2: Different behavior with countrymen	I would have behaved differently if the person would have been a fellow countryman
ST5.3: Foreigner should be more careful	The person should have been more careful in dealing with me, because of his/her foreign origin while being in my country
ST5.4: Problem related to his origin	The peculiar behavior of the person was related to his/her cultural origin
ST5.5: Behavior was expected due to his origin	His/her behavior was on expected lines in keeping with his/her specific foreign origin

PART 3: (Demographic Questions - General)

Country of Residence	Present Country of Residence
Region	Geographical Region
City of Residence	Present City of Residence
Age	Age
Residential Status	Residential Status
Education Level	Education Level
Income Group	Income Group

Another set of brainstorming sessions and focus group discussions were based on the investigation of 'level of CFC' in the national context involving cultural differences at the sub culture's level. Following theoretical accounts were the basis of such discussion.

Level of comfort with 'culturally different'

In the national context, taking an example of cultural diversity of a large country like *India*, workplace diversity in large national and international companies can be very stark, especially in large *Indian* cities like *Mumbai*, *Delhi*, *Bangalore* and others. *India*, for example, is religiously most diverse nation in the world. According to a 2002 census of *India*, the religion of 80% of the people is *Hinduism*. *Islam* is practiced by around 13%. There are over 23 million *Christians*, over 19 million *Sikhs*, about 8 million *Buddhists* and about 4 million *Jains* in the country. Apart from the persons of foreign origins working with the local people, people from far flung *Indian* provinces, with diverse cultural backgrounds are part of the workforce.

Culturally they may be quite different from the local or regional cultures they work. For example, consider a KPO workplace in Bangalore, where persons of overseas origin are working with natives, people from north of *India*, from *West Bengal, Odessa, Maharashtra, Kerala, Jammu and Kashmir* etc. This may make managing such diverse workforce a daunting task for team managers.

However, it is also a fact that while persons of *Indian* origin carry with them a common *Indian* culture which is the result of an ancient common history, similarities of religion, food habits, consuming of common types of goods and services, *Bollywood*, common style of politics, common problems, common education system, etc., they represent different religions, different superstitions, different styles of lifestyles and different weather conditions they have lived in for a large part of their life. It would be interesting to study how these differences and similarities operate in multi - cultural workplaces in large corporations in major *Indian* cities. For the purpose of this book, culturally different persons included all those culturally different persons belong to far flung cultures and even those with foreign origins. The same is true for similarly large countries like *Italy, Portugal, US, China* and others.

India's diversity has inspired many *Indian* and foreign writers to publish their perspectives to country's culture. These writings paint a complicated and often conflicting picture of the cultural diversity of *India*. According to industry consultant *Eugene M. Makar*, for example, traditional *Indian* culture is characterized by a relatively strict social hierarchy. He also mentions that it is a common social practice that from an early age, children are reminded of their roles and places in society[33]. What many believe about gods and spirits, have an integral and functional role in determining their life. Several differences such as religion and rituals divide the cultures. Strict social taboos have governed *Hindu* religion's bifurcation of menial and non menial jobs in society, for thousands of years. However in recent years, particularly in large *Indian* cities, some of these lines of work divisions, have blurred and sometimes even disappeared. *Makar* further writes that important family relations extend as far as *Gotra*, the mainly patrilineal lineage or clan assigned to a *Hindu* at birth. In rural areas & sometimes in urban areas as well, it is common that three or four generations of the family live under the same roof. The patriarch often resolves family issues. These manifestations of culture spills over to the workplaces in *Indian* businesses to some extent and plays in important role in shaping the HR practices at work places even in big organizations operating from larger cities.

There are other perceptions of *Indian* culture as well. According to an interview with *C.K. Prahalad* by *Des Dearlove* (2009)[34], author of many best selling business books, modern *India* is a multicultural country with diverse cultures and with different languages, religions and traditions. Children begin their educational life, by coping and learning to accept and assimilate in this diversity of cultures. *Prahalad* - who was born in *India* and grew up there - claimed, in the interview, that *Indians*, like everyone else in the world, want to be treated as unique, as individuals, want to express them and seek innovation[34].

In another report, *Nancy Lockwood* (2009)[35] writes that in the past two decades or so, there has been a dramatic change in social structure in *India* in direct contrast to the expectations from traditional *Indian* culture. These changes have resulted in *Indian* families, giving educational opportunities to girls, accepting women working outside the home, pursuing a career, and opening the possibility for women to attain managerial roles in corporate *India*. *Lockwood* claims that while change is slow, the scale of cultural change can be sensed from the fact that of *India*'s 397 million workers, 124 million are now women.

The issues in *India* with women empowerment are similar to that elsewhere in the world[39]. According to *Sen, A* (2005)[36], the culture of modern *India* is a complex blend of its historical traditions, influences from the effects of colonialism over centuries and current western culture - both collaterally and dialectically[40]. Based on the focus group discussions and *Delphi* sessions on the similar lines as done in the international context, a set of directly observable variables was finalized for the national context as given in the table 6.1a (see CCD questionnaire in Annexure).

Concluding from the above exercises and discussions, it can be said that CFC can be fully understood through a deeper study (of the type discussed in this book) taking cues from the contemporary society and organizational culture theories. Further studies also suggest that a new level of cultural sensitivities, abilities and competencies can be developed through a correct understanding of cross cultural comfort dynamics in multicultural teams. This should go a long way in deriving maximum benefits of having multicultural work teams in multinational enterprises. As far as the explanation of the level of comfort with foreign cultures is concerned, above theory forms a strong basis to build concept and construct to define observed variables of cross cultural comfort. These variables can be tested for their goodness of fit to the explanation of dependant exogenous variable, i.e. factors of level of comfort with foreign cultures (CFC). The same process has been used in building comfort with foreign cultures (CFC) models in the later sections of this book.

These studies also provide specific latent variables which give concepts to certain important directly observable variables which can form a basis for survey instrument required for any quantitative investigation for the above understanding. Some of these variables relate to societal stereotypes, patriotism, religion effect, personal ease of working with foreigners, societal attitudes towards foreigners etc. At the same time, the current chapter throws important light on the approach to such investigation, especially in the context of *Hofstede*'s approach to such investigation and understanding of how society behaves in the presence of internal and external factors affecting society's attitude.

The same societal behavior model had been used in this study to come out with the survey instrument, overall categorization of effective variables, control variables and latent variables, with the use of qualitative and quantitative approach to empirical investigation. Apart from a discussion on several cross cultural variables identified through literature review, a healthy discussion on differences in value systems of different regions of the world also provided an insight on the structure and process of 'level of CFC' which is the focus of this book. *Hofstede*'s account of the reaction of the local culture to foreign cultures also provided a good starting point for the studies discussed in this book, which had been widely used by the research volunteers, especially during the brain storming sessions on the practical structure of a suitable survey instrument. During the preliminary study stage also much of the existing literature as discussed in this chapter came very handy in forming a perception on national cultures and societal behavior.

Conclusion

This chapter has successfully discussed and identified the directly observed cultural factors or variables which can be theoretically and empirically tested for their impact on the 'level of CFC'. These variables also have the potential to produce and help identify a limited set of most important latent variables which may describe the phenomenon of 'level of CFC' in a more scientific way. The identified variables are also suitable for a secondary and primary study of 'level of CFC'.

Suggested questions for discussion:

1) Discuss the differences between the terms – stereotypes, prejudice and discrimination. Give examples.
2) How does cultural background of the consumers impact their choice of products and services? Discuss with examples.
3) Do you think there is any connection between 'culture' and 'desire

to explore' among people? Discuss with examples.

4) Do you think people with different national cultures may have different views about the 'merits of globalization'? Discuss with examples.

5) Is there any evidence to the fact that there could be differences in values and belief of different cultures of the world? How do these differences impact organizations and projects? Discuss

6) Do you think cultural differences within nations can also impact organizations the way national differences does? Discuss with examples.

Notes:

1. Fiske, Susan T., Lee, & Tiane L. (2008). *'Stereotypes and prejudice create workplace discrimination'*. In Brief, Arthur P. Diversity at Work. New York: Cambridge University Press. pp. 13–52. ISBN 978-0-521-86030-7.

2. House, R.J. & Javidan, M. (2004). Overview of GLOBE. In R. J. House, P.J. Hanges, M. Javidan, P. W. Dorfman, V. Gupta (Eds.), *Culture, leadership and organizations*. The GLOBE study of 62 societies (pp. 9-28). Thousand Oaks, CA: Sage Publications.

3. Marquardt, M.J., and Kearsley G. (1999). *Technology based learning: Maximizing Human Performance and Corporate Success*, St. Lucie Press, Boca Raton

4. Kohls, L.R. (1981). *Developing Intercultural Awareness: A learning Module Complete with Master Lesson Plan, Contents, Exercises and Handouts*, The Society of Intercultural Education, Training and Research, Washington DC

5. Norris, P. & Inglehart, Ronald (2004). *Sacred and Secular: Religion and Politics Worldwide.*, New York and Cambridge: Cambridge University Press.

6. Fiske, Susan T. (1998). *"Stereotyping, Prejudice, and Discrimination"*. In Gilbert, Daniel T.; Fiske, Susan T.; Lindzey, Gardner. The Handbook of Social Psychology. Volume Two (4th ed.). Boston, Mass.: McGraw-Hill. p. 357. ISBN 978-0-19-521376-8.

7. Denmark, Florence L. (2010). *"Prejudice and Discrimination"*. In Weiner, Irving B.; Craighead, W. Edward. The Corsini Encyclopedia of Psychology. Volume Three (4th ed.). Hoboken, N.J.: John Wiley. p. 1277.

8. Tajfel, Henri (1981). *"Social stereotypes and social groups"*. In Turner, John C.; Giles, Howard. Intergroup behavior. Oxford: Blackwell. pp. 144–167.ISBN 978-0-631-11711-7.

9. Katz, Daniel, Braly & Kenneth W. (1935). "Racial prejudice and racial stereotypes". *The Journal of Abnormal and Social Psychology* (American Psychological Association) 30 (2): 175–193. doi:10.1037/h0059800.

10. Cox, William T. L., Abramson, Lyn Y., Devine, Patricia G. & Hollon, Steven D. (2012) "Stereotypes, Prejudice, and Depression: The Integrated Perspective". *Perspectives on Psychological Science.* 7 (5): 427–449.

11. Tilcsik, András, 2011). "Pride and Prejudice: Employment Discrimination against Openly Gay Men in the United States". *American Journal of Sociology* 117 (2): 586–626.

12. Sinclair, Stacey, Hardin, Curtis D. & Lowery, Brian S. (2006). "Self-Stereotyping in the Context of Multiple Social Identities". *Journal of Personality and Social Psychology* (American Psychological Association) 90 (4): 529–542

13. Correll, J., Park, B., Judd, Charles M. & Wittenbrink, B. (2002). "The Police Officer's Dilemma: Using Ethnicity to Disambiguate Potentially Threatening Individuals". *Journal of Personality and Social Psychology.* 83 (6)

14. Levitt, Theodore (1983). The Globalization of Markets, *Harvard Business Review*, 61 (May-June), pp. 92-102.

15. Klein, J., Ettenson, R, and Morris, M, (1998), "The Animosity Model of Eoreign Produce Purchase: An Empirical Test in the Peoples' Republic of *China*", *Journal of Marketing*, 62, pp. 89-100.

16. Shimp, T and Sharma, S., (1987), "Consumer Ethnocentrism: Construction and Validation of the CETSCALE", *Journal of Marketing Research*, 23, pp, 280-9,

17. Franken, R. (1994). *Human motivation* (3rd ed.). Brooks/Cole Publishing Co., Pacific Grove, CA.

18. Berlyne, D.E. (1960) *Conflict, Arousal, and Curiosity.* New York: McGraw Hill.

19. Langevin, R. (1971). Is curiosity a unitary construct? *Canadian Journal of Psychology*, (25) 360-374.

20. Fowler, H. (1965). *Curiosity and Exploratory Behavior.* New York: Macmillan.

21. Helling, C.S., and Dragun, J.1981. *Test Protocols for Environmental fate and movement of Toxicants*, Association of Official analytical chemists; Arlington, Va.

22. Zuckerman, M. (1994). *Behavioral Expressions and Biosocial Bases of Sensation Seeking.* New York: Cambridge University Press.

23. Ervin, J. & Smith Z.A. (2008). *Globalization: A Reference Handbook. ABC-CLIO.* p. 35. ISBN 978-1-59884-073-5

24. Jennings, J. (2010). *Globalizations and the Ancient World.* Cambridge University Press. p. 132. ISBN 978-0-521-76077-5. Retrieved 4 February 2013.

25. Barker, C. (2008). *Cultural Studies: Theory and Practice.* SAGE. pp. 159–162. ISBN 978-1-4129-2416-0.

26. O'Connor, D.E. (2006). *Encyclopedia of the Global Economy A Guide For Students and Researchers.* Academic Foundation. pp. 391–. ISBN 978-81-7188-547-3. Retrieved 4 February 2013

27. Kirby, M. (2000). *Sociology in Perspective. Heinemann.* pp. 407–408.ISBN 978-0-435-33160-3. Retrieved 4 February 2013.

28. Willis, K. (2013). *Theories of Development*, Routledge, London

29. Kramarae, C & Spender, D. (2000). *Routledge International Encyclopedia of Women: Global Women's Issues and Knowledge.* Taylor & Francis. pp. 933–.ISBN 978-0-415-92088-9. Retrieved 4 February 2013

30. Hiramoto, M. (2012). *Media Intertextualities.* John Benjamins Publishing. p. 76. ISBN 978-90-272-0256-7. Retrieved 4 February 2013

31. Norris, P. & Inglehart, Ronald (2004). *Sacred and Secular: Religion and Politics Worldwide., New York and Cambridge*: Cambridge University Press.

32. Hofstede, G. (2001). *Culture's consequences: Comparing values, behaviors, institutions, and organizations across nations.* Thousand Oaks, CA: Sage.

33. Makar, EM (2008). *An American guide to doing business in India*, published by Adams Business

34. Dearlove, D. (2009). "On the verge of something extraordinary". *Business Strategy Review*, London Business School: 17–20

35. Lockwood, N. (2009). *Perspectives on Women in Management in India.* Society for Human Resource Management

36. Sen, A. (2005). *The Argumentative Indian: Writings on Indian History, Culture and Identity.* Penguin Books. ISBN 978-0-312-42602-6

Online resources for this chapter, available at:
http://www.vijeshjain.com/books/multinational-workplaces/resources/chapter-6

7. CONCEPTUAL CFC MODEL

In this part of the book, a methodology has been described which was used to hunt for a simple preliminary conceptual preliminary model for CFC. A process of 'perception scaling and consultative process' had been used to first identify direct observable parameters (the same has been described in an earlier chapter) which can be studied and scored using secondary data and published information. Later the same process was used with the help of a set of cross cultural experts and focus groups to evaluate published information and score the countries on CFC scores. List of country studies also was finalized using the same process. Excerpts of secondary information used in scoring the countries on the conceptual CFC model are also shared in this chapter.

This part of the preliminary study looked into the phenomenon of CFC in multinational firms, based on qualitative societal differences among different nations. The preliminary study conceptually and qualitatively identified several 'comfort variables' which may impact 'CFC' among team members. The objective of this part of the study was to measure the impact of these variables on CFC using qualitative country data and to study whether 'level of CFC' varies significantly among country to country. While this preliminary study was not exhaustive and final in its nature, it nevertheless provided a good starting point to study the variation of 'level of CFC' of local cultures (inter country) with foreign cultures in international project teams in multinational firms and covered a good number of countries.

CFC is a phenomenon which can be understood from primarily two perspectives. One perspective is to look at the different societal cultures having different propensity to feel at ease with foreign cultures or with the people who are culturally different due to certain combined effect of the society's overall opinion and behavior which may be the result of common local history, local political views and experiences, dominant religious sentiments etc. Another perspective is related to psychological factors associated with each individual belonging to a particular society which decides how he or she behave at work place. Although at the organizational level, organization culture plays an important role in how employees behave on the job and in the cross cultural teams.

The main objective of this part of the study was to look into the societal perspective which could be measured through published data. This data, for example, related to giving an insight into things like how immigrants feel in an alien nation, how they are generally treated by the host people, host government, their host employers and by their colleagues at their workplace in host countries. The parameters of these types could be measured using published data related to several countries from different sources, like online forums, articles on expatriates, articles and research work of political and social journalists, country profiles, etc. Although there are several conceptual models derived with this approach and relate to, for example 'ease of doing business in different countries', however, most of these models deal with commercial aspect of doing business and the level of freedom a country provides legally to foreign investors, companies operating in host countries for procedural ease point of view. These researches have not touched upon the idea of dealing with 'people's issues' associated with ease of doing business, or how much the local people feel comfortable with culturally different people providing a cosmopolitan environment in which foreigners feel at home and thrive in their professions in host countries? This part of the book looked into such issues and explained the methods adopted to find a preliminary framework as well as the techniques used to create a preliminary CFC model using published data with a qualitative approach.

In this part of the study a preliminary framework was postulated with the help of which countries could be scored on their 'level of comfort with foreign cultures'. The scientific research method for this research was designed to be through 'perception scaling and consultative' process. The process was motivated by the studies conducted by *Geert Hofstede* (1980)[1] and others. In order to postulate a preliminary CFC model using the data from published sources (collected during the process between its stages 2 and 3 (as explained in a later section), expert groups were formed, involving around 200 experts and a selected set of students of cross culture courses. They were clustered into 10 focus groups for above process. The authors along with a few experts acted as the facilitators for the 10 focus groups which were formed. A list of selected countries to be part of this study, parameters which form the CFC model and weights assigned to each parameter was also finalized through this consultative process using *the Delphi technique* of stage wise elimination process by the focus groups. Figure 7.1 gives a pictorial view of the research design and methodology used in this part of the research.

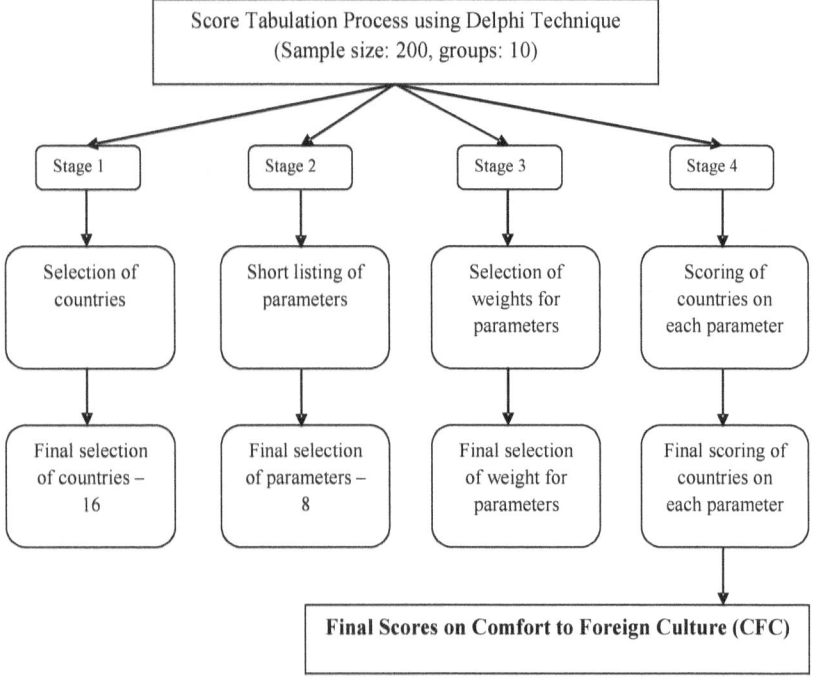

Figure 7.1: Research design for obtaining CFC model

Data Collection

After stage 2 and before stage 3 as described in a later section, a collection of 'data and information' was carried out in the selected countries. The information was collected mainly from published sources. The information was systematically categorized according to eight parameters as resulted from Stage 2 and organized for easy access in one central place, so that opinions could be formed using specific information from the expert focus groups. The nature and form of information generated from the research were varied. A sample of selected country wise information collected for the research is given below.

France

France is a fairly multicultural society. Large cities, universities and science - all of it live and feed off the cultural diversity this country has to offer. Out of the 59.9 million living here, an estimated 4.2 million are foreigners. Out of these 4.2 million, about 45% are *African* or *North African*, 40% are *European* and 12% are *Asian*. *French* culture is not homogeneous. Diversity is evident everywhere and at all times. Curiously, at the same time, various characteristics of the different ways of life are quite attached to different local areas. The language, food and customs vary from region to region, which can make adapting to the country a little harder if a foreigner plans on staying in various different places in this country. As in many parts of the world, in *France* one may find a few that aren't very welcoming to foreigners; one may find that locals will be more inclined to help if the foreigner try speaking some *French* or at least ask if they happen to speak *English*, instead of simply addressing them in *English*. Courtesy is always appreciated.

Muslims make up a considerable part of *French* society. Of the 3.5 million *Muslims* currently residing in *France*, half a million of these are *French* citizens. There have been recent tensions between the *Muslims* and *Non Muslim* population in *France*, especially after some of the terrorist attacks were carried out by a few fundamentalists and subsequently the banning of head scarves in public schools, a measure introduced by the *French* education minister. While government attitude towards immigrants has been positive in the past, there are still several checks and balances in the *French* policy towards allowing foreign workers and businessmen. Of course bureaucracy has been a major hurdle in attracting large and useful immigrant population in the country.

Every law in *France* is made in such a way as to make it easy for the 'Euro work card holders'. The rules generally are such as to allow decent living and enjoyable stay for them in *France*. Workers from other countries find it difficult to adjust to the laws applicable to the foreign workers in *France*, especially for those who are married and their spouses wishing to live in *France*. In addition, most of the work visa applications from nationals from non *EU* countries are processed on a case to case basis severely negating the transparency in the work visa process. In general, foreigners face different treatment from the *French* consulate depending upon whether they originate from *EU* countries, or countries with which *France* has signed treaties for establishment (like *the US*) on one hand, and other countries on which *France* has rigorous controls to grant work visas (most of the other countries) on the other.

Poland

Polish People are highly educated, tolerant and they like the change. They are ready to experiment with new things and generally accept the foreigners. While many *Polish* natives left the country in search of better careers, still many foreigners came to *Poland* for many of its good things including its highly interesting and inviting culture. *Poland* is not a highly multicultural society with a very less *Muslim* population, the majority being ardent *Catholics*, but it has high quality of culture and people are very friendly to the foreigners. The population is highly homogenous with 96.5 population being *Polish*. *Poland* is generally not at all racist, although football matches have shown racist tendencies from some isolated cases according to a recent report[2].

United States

Traditionally an 'immigration country', *USA* is supposed to be the number one choice for immigrants from the world. In 2005, total immigrant population in *the US* had been reported at around 40 million. While still retaining the number one choice as a work and business destination, *US* immigration and work rules have been drastically tightened up after the 9/11. The recession of 2008, had also brought insecurities among the native population and till recently there was a general mood in *the US* against the new foreigners entering the country. President *Obama* met with 30 congressional leaders on June 25, 2009 to begin "an honest discussion about the issues" involved in comprehensive immigration reforms. *Obama* said the goal was to identify "areas of agreement and areas where we still have work to do, with the hope of beginning the debate in earnest later this year" [3]. The government policy of *US* towards immigrants generally have related to the varying attitudes of the respective presidents of *US* on the issue.

China

Before mid 1980s, *China* was termed as an 'isolated, mysterious country' by the foreigners who visited this country, because most foreigners were forbidden to freely move in *China*'s mainland and had to confine themselves to certain designated places and hotels. After mid 1980s, the *Chinese* government's attitude changed towards making foreigners live and enjoy in *China* relatively freely. However the restrictions are still there on how foreigners live in *China*. The 'green card' scheme, short term and long term residence permits, are now much more acceptable forms of living in *China* for the foreigners[4].

As far as the common people of *China* are concerned, they have a 'love and hate' relationship with foreigners[5]. While an average *Chinese* want to learn *English*, travel abroad, and see *Hollywood* movies, they get irritated by ordinary street incidents involving foreigners in their country. The main reason of such behavior is the uncomfortable historical events involving foreigners in *China* and the tendency of the *Chinese* government to inflame nationalist feelings constantly to justify its own legitimacy as the *communist* regime of the land. The attitude of the *Chinese* government can be gauged from the fact that hardly any blog or forum discussing life of foreigners in *China* is active on the internet within the country since the state machinery is working constantly to block any such free expressions of thoughts by the public on the internet, at least for viewing in *China*.

Germany

No *German* thinks of their country as a country of immigrants like *US* and *Canada*. And no demographic or social issue has generated a bigger controversy than the issue of the presence of foreigners in their country. This is despite the fact, that the contributions of the immigrant population in *Germany* to the economic growth of the country is among the highest and they also pay more in taxes than natives. Their removal from *Germany* may be catastrophic for the overall health of its economy. *German* laws are not very much to the comfort of the foreigners working and living there. Foreign population is not distributed evenly in the country.

Denmark

While on paper *Denmark* has certain schemes and programs for the much needed foreign skills in their country, for example the much touted 'green card scheme' (2009)[6]. In reality, general mood of the *Danes* is against the foreigners. They routinely and openly express their dismay towards the foreigner's entry into *Denmark*[7]. They generally feel that the foreigners are exploiting the social security system built on the taxes paid by them as evident from the multiple comments posted on the website, 'ForeignersinDenmark.dk' (2009)[8]. They even feel that foreigners are to be blamed for the increasing crimes in *Denmark* or simply they are alien to the country and should leave the country for good. Interestingly rules made in *Denmark* for the foreigners married to *Danes* are such that it makes it difficult for their spouses to settle in *Denmark*. Moreover, for immigrants, it is hard to compete in a job market uninterested in employing foreigners/immigrants.

This is also the plea taken by *Denmark* politicians against an elaborate system of social security of the new immigrants. The government's attitude towards foreign immigrants is now increasingly becoming representative of the majority of *the Danish population*. Immigrants now need to live in

Denmark for seven years and not three years as was the earlier rule, to get citizenship. Most non - refugee immigrants can't collect welfare cheques immediately on entering the country. No one in the country can bring a foreigner spouse less than 24 years of age. *Denmark* has been receiving a poorer rating around the world on their secularist credentials and racism record too.

Hungary

Hungary is a country having a non radical approach, unlike the *West European* countries where people look upon the foreigners as the problem creators of uncontrollable type. In *Hungary*, foreigners are well accepted and are part and parcel of their day to day life. Not very long ago, when more and more *Chinese* started settling in *Budapest*, initially natives thought of them as '*Chinese* Invaders' ("Foreigners in *Hungary*," 2005)[9]. But when natives closely looked at their ways and lifestyles, they found that they mostly set up new enterprises with *Chinese* goods available at affordable prices. While *European Union* (*EU*) nationals are not considered foreigners after *Hungary* entered the *EU*, others find that government regulates their life in *Hungary* in some ways. For every purchase of property in *Hungary*, a foreigner requires government permission.

People in *Hungary* are generally very friendly, but they initially shy away from foreigners. One of the major reasons is that most foreigners are relatively richer than average *Hungarians* and their motives of being in *Hungary* are mostly to spend money and have fun (since a large number of foreigners enter the country as tourist for very short stays), which is quite different from what a *Hungarian* likes to do. So they remain unfriendly to the foreigners initially, but once a foreigner proves that he is not of the type of the stereotype of the above kind, and he is sincere in his work and he means business, *Hungarian* shower lots of warmth and friendliness. Historically *Hungarians* have a very bitter history and most *Hungarians* are serious about their career and lifestyle. They save lots of money for hard times and work hard. *Hungary* is a truly secular country and being at the center of *Europe* offers a land of varied heritage of religions. However, being from the communist era, *Hungarians* are not very religious people and do not adhere to a specific religion. Religious freedom is guaranteed by the constitution.

Iran

Iranians are generally very warm to strangers, including foreigners, although *Iranian* government has frequently and officially declared western countries as their opponents and even its enemies. Most foreigners are welcomed by the common people and bureaucratic hurdles for the foreigners to work and live in *Iran* are almost negligible, albeit foreigners need to adhere to certain *Islamic* norms. A vast *Diaspora* of *Iran* works abroad for better income whilst a large refugee population exists at home[10].

Japan

Japanese culture is one of the most misunderstood cultures in the world. In order to understand the *Japanese* culture one must live in *Japan* and with *Japanese* people for a very long time. In fact, most of the common '*Hofstede* scores' in the cultural dimensions need to be corrected and updated in the light of this fact. As for the foreigner's issues, *Japanese* people are very much positive to foreigners, although most foreigners find them extreme racist, as having a superiority complex and doing things their own way without accepting the foreign ways as evident from the multiple comments posted on *Namiko's Japanese* Language Blog (2009)[11]. The truth is far from this. Those who closely understand the *Japanese* culture will tell you that most *Japanese* are shy by nature, they rather have kind of inferiority complex while with foreigners and they fear having been misunderstood by *English* speaking foreigners.

However, the government immigration laws are very much in disfavor of the foreigners and are very strict. One of the reasons for this situation, given by some experts is that a section of the *Japanese* people and the *Japanese* government conclude that foreigners are responsible for the majority of the crimes in *Japan*. For this reason, even a permanent foreign resident of *Japan* are fingerprinted on every entry into *Japan. Japanese* society is a highly homogeneous society with very less cultural diversity due to several historical reasons. This situation also makes the life of foreigners difficult in *Japan*. Several experts say that in its present state, *Japan* is the best place to live for the *Japanese* people and not for the foreigners. Religious freedom in *Japan* is one more problem area. In spite of high economic development, religious tolerance in *Japan* is still in its infancy. "*Americans* have a long tradition of the separation of the two entities (read religion and state), but that distinction, despite the postwar constitution, does not exist in the *Japanese* culture[12]". Unfortunately the religious tolerance in *Japan*, as a trend, is gradually on the decline mainly due to the absence of a developed civil liberty system and a lack of judicial independence to oppose the state's encroachment on the religious matters of its subjects.

Having one of the lowest immigrant populations, *Japan* has very strict immigration laws designed to make foreigners feel very uncomfortable in the long run. Employers have a complex system of recruitment, having an informal system of 'connections' to fill its jobs, normally shying away to recruit foreigners in their companies.

South Korea

In *South Korea*, Foreigners are allotted unique identification numbers (ARC-alien's registration card) which differentiate them from the local people. Due to heavy dependence of *Korean* life on online services, all residents need to use these identification numbers frequently to get several day to day services. Strangely, most of these services are out of bounds for the foreigners since these programs do not recognize the ARC numbers. Therefore, they can never be part of the *South Korean* life completely even if they have lived there for several years. The situation is so bad that ARC holders with valid working visas are unable to get the mobile phone account even after spending 4 years in *South Korea*. A similar problem exists to get credit cards and sometimes a bank account. In fact, there is only one bank in *South Korea*, which offers credit cards to foreign residents. The government has announced certain policy changes to correct this situation and to offer comfort to the foreigners in *South Korea*, but these measures are too little and too slow. *South Korea* in its real sense is not a multicultural society, although it may be called as multiethnic society. However, *South Korea* is among world's most pluralist and religiously tolerant society. [13]

South Africa

"The Hate is Back" (25th July, 2009)[14] proclaimed the headline of one of *South Africa's* leading newspapers after foreigners were once again targeted with violence sweeping through townships across the country. Several foreigners have fled the scene of violence across the country. Anger is mounting in this country against the foreigners. While *South Africa (SA)* is a multicultural, multi ethnic country and the government has a declared policy towards foreigner's tolerance, non racialism and cultural freedom, these policies have largely failed on the ground level. The government has adopted a bureaucratic framework to accommodate the concerns of foreigners living in *South Africa*. These are good initiatives by the Government[15]. Two third of the population of *South Africa* is *Christian*. According to the International Religious Freedom Report on *SA*, (2007)[16], the *SA* constitution provides for religious freedom and government generally respects this right in practice. There are no reports of societal abuses or discrimination based on religious belief or practice, in the recent times.

SA is often called as a complex racial and culture, theatre when compared with other countries in the world. At workplaces, for the most part, *South Africans* want to maintain harmonious working relationships, so they avoid confrontations, as cited in *South Africa* - Language, Culture, Customs and Etiquette (2009)[17]

Tanzania

Many observers consider *Tanzania* to be among very few countries with long standing history of religious harmony, especially between two major religious groups – *Muslims* (around 25%) and *Christians* (around 75%)[18]. Other observers think differently with a view of the relationship between the two major religions as involving rivalry and conflict, consequently socioeconomic and political problems are given religious expressions. Inequalities and injustice are now viewed through a religious angle. *Tanzania* is home to a patterned cultural mosaic of over 120 distinct ethnic groups, united in peaceful coexistence under one country, one language and one flag. There is no history of civil unrest, ethnic tensions, political dictatorship or religious intolerance.

India

Cultural diversity of *India* is the result of cultural mingling of different groups for thousands of years. People lived in *India* even during *Stone Age*. The years of foreign colonial rule, religious movements, and spiritual discoveries in the ancient land of *India* have given it a potpourri of religions unmatched anywhere in the world. Virtually every religion in the world has a connection with *India* in its present state.[19] While foreigners visiting *India* can face a multitude of problems including violent crimes, *Indian* culture is not entirely against foreigners and generally they are welcome and feel comfortable if they understand in advance the ways and means of surviving on *Indian* soil. Historically, though, *India* has its own share of several foreign 'invasions and aggressions', which has made *Indian* people generally suspicious of foreigners, especially towards *Europeans*. However, this suspicion does not impact very much on the day to day life of foreigners, in relatively bigger cities, who wish to work and do business in *India* for short term or even long term. Being a predominantly major tourist destination, *India*'s common people are generally sensitive about the warm *Indian* hospitality ('guests are god') which is expected by the foreigners in *India* and which is generally appreciated world over.

New Zealand

In spite of a good quality living and a laid back lifestyle, *Kiwis* are not very tolerant of other races specially *Chinese*, *Indians* and other *Asians*. Compared to *Australia* and *Canada*, getting a work visa and a residency visa for *New Zealand* is much easier. Racism is very high among the residents. A new survey has found that "more than 90 percent of *non-Europeans* in '*Nelson*' region have experienced some form of racial abuse," ranging from "verbal attacks to violence that has resulted in prosecution." Initiated in *Canada*, picked up in *Australia* in 1970s, the concept of multiculturalism was quickly spread to *New Zealand*. 23% of the total population being foreign born from around the world, *New Zealand* is a highly multicultural country. Immigrants continue to make *New Zealand* more multicultural. Many of *New Zealand's* immigrants are of *Polynesian* descent and have come to join families or find safety from political corruption from their native islands. Many *Asians* are studying in the cities and there are many from *Britain* who came to find a change in lifestyle.

Australia

Australia is a country of immigrants similar to *the US*, *Canada* and *New Zealand*. Generally people are warm and they welcome foreigners. But it is often said that if you are not an *Asian*, or an *Indian* student or a *Muslim*, you are welcome in *Australia*. These remarks are quite true to the country. Recent spurt in street attacks on *Asians*, *particularly Indian* students is the demonstration of how true these remarks are. The *UN* has recently warned that some of the 'immigrant' countries, it is likely that immigrants and refugees may be made the scapegoat for the economic downturn and may even be attacked.[20] ("UN says," 2009). *Australia* seems to be the country where this seems to be already happening. Even the immigration policies of *Australia* are looking for change as a reaction to the economic downturn. An 11-year study into 'Racism in *Australia*' by a collaboration of *Australian* universities found that 85 per cent of *Australians* acknowledge that racial prejudice occurs in the nation with one in five claiming to be a victim of racist verbal abuse or related incidents.

Canada

Canada is an immigration nation and is popular internationally as one of the best places in the world for the foreigners. However, it is highly debated status given to this country for a number of persons having mixed bags of experiences in *Canada*. While most immigrants complain they are unable to get jobs in their own field of specialization and several qualified people end up doing menial jobs there, the fact is that immigration to *Canada* is highly publicized and there are long queues of the people from around the world wishing to immigrate to *Canada*. The number of people immigrating to *Canada* is also one of the highest in the world. One of the most common complaints of the new immigrants to *Canada*, *especially* those who could not find better work profiles there, is that *the Canadian Government* has some archaic rules and regulations which forces many to look for subsistence level jobs. Many doctors, engineers and even PhDs, educated overseas, end up doing jobs like taxi driving, pizza deliveries, security & neighborhood watch, especially in their initial years in *Canada* after landing there as permanent residents. It is also alleged whole immigration system of *Canada* is discriminatory, time taking and is not transparent. Many have even suggested that the whole system is a money making strategy of the *Canadian* Government. In spite of all these negative feedback from the immigrants, *the Canadian people* are not averse to foreigners and are religiously very tolerant. In spite of being an immigration country, *Canada* is not generally regarded as multicultural and it is said that *American* culture is dominant here.

Switzerland

Switzerland is a highly multicultural society, although most of the ethnic groups originate from the *European* cultures only. There are major cultural differences among different *German* speaking and *Italian* speaking 'cantons'. Language, economic, climatic, educational and religious differences exist among these cantons. Although the natives are quite reserved in their nature, they do not quite really welcome the foreigners. They are very punctual and straight forward with anyone, including the foreigners. The political structure is highly decentralized, in order to accommodate different ethnic groups and to allow them to resolve their differences by governing themselves.

However, even when the society at large denounces right wing terrorism, a large section of *Swiss* population has been accused of being racist in the international as well as national media. This is one of the conclusions of a study presented by the National Research Program (NRP 40+) on right-wing extremism in *Switzerland*, on 24 February 2009. During his visit in January 2006, the *United Nations* special *Rapporteur* on racism, *Doudou Diène*, had observed that *Switzerland* suffers from racism, discrimination and xenophobia.

The methodology used for deriving conceptual CFC model

As mentioned earlier, the scientific research method for this part of the research was designed to be through 'perception scaling and consultative' process. In order to get insights from the collected data, expert focus groups were formed with 200 members, involving experts and a selected set of students of cross culture courses. They were clustered into 10 groups for above process. All the group members were briefed on the research process, research objectives and were asked to come prepared with the pre study of literature review related to the enquiry of this research (on the lines of what is described earlier). Further collected information on several selected countries was made available to all the members as and when it was required.

The process went in four stages. In Stage 1, a limited set of countries was to be finalized for the study representing competing cultures and different representative countries of several geographical areas of the world. This selection was also based on the core objectives of the study. The objective of selection was announced in the form of a question which was–

"Which are the countries likely to represent major cultures of the world and are representative of a wider section of the inhabitants of this planet?"

Ten groups were asked to reply to each of these questions, giving reasons of their selection of ranks of countries based on their importance to the inquiry. The countries selected for ranking were 30 in number and the list was discussed with each group for their significance to the core objectives. In the iteration process, summary of decisions of all groups with their respective reasons for selection were presented, anonymously.

The consultative and discussion process led the other groups to modify their preferences in subsequent rounds, based on anonymous views worked out for each group. When there was a near consensus among all the groups with respect to rank the scores (1 to 30) to major countries this phase of iteration was stopped. The selection of countries to be included in the study could be obtained by studying the means of the rank scores given by each group for each possible country out of 30 initially selected. After 10th round, each of the groups converged into 'ranking choices of countries' and 'optimum number of countries to be studied'. The group unanimously decided to include 22 countries in the study.

In Stage 2, *Delphi* groups were asked to identify the most appropriate parameters which nearly reflected the phenomenon of CFC, 24 initial parameters were identified by expert groups. These parameters were debated for their relevance and importance to the construct. Initial 24 parameters were debated by the groups in different rounds and objective questions were asked to be debated and answered, attaching importance scores to each parameter. The iteration process summarized the results of each group, anonymously, with the explanation of the reasons for the selection of more important parameters over others by each group. After each round, every group was prompted to reconsider scores on the importance of parameters based on such briefing of results of the previous rounds. At the end of 8th iteration, a set of eight parameters could be converged to be most important out of total of initial 24 parameters. Also the 'importance score' of each of eight parameters (1 to 10) was significantly higher as indicated unanimously by each of the group.

It is to be noted that the mean importance scores were summarized for all the groups in each round. In the last round (8th Round) importance scores for most important eight parameters nearly matched for each group. 'Importance scores' were based on the following question –

"Which parameters reflect (or provide insights) most closely to the enquiry of the level of comfort of a local culture with the foreign culture i.e. Comfort with Foreign Culture (CFC)?"

After stage 2 and before stage 3, collection of 'data and information' was carried out on the 22 selected countries. Information was collected from several sources, including newspapers, countries specific web sites, related blogs and forums, country information books, travelogues, country specific published researches, government bulletins, journalistic articles, views of experts on particular countries etc. The information was systematically categorized according to eight parameters as resulted from Stage 2 and organized for easy access at one central place, so that opinions could be formed using specific information by the expert groups.

In Stage 3, fresh *Delphi* groups, formed again, discussed and identified weights which were given to the identified final eight parameters that could be used to measure CFC scores. The question given to these ten groups was

What is the level of contribution of each selected parameter to final CFC scores?

At the end of 5th iteration, final set of weights could be arrived at. In this final round, weights given by each group nearly converged to the final weights agreed by each group.

Thereafter, in the stage 4, new groups among 200 experts were formed to suggest scores for each of the eight parameters using the categorized information collected between stages two and three. In a total of five iterations, scores were analyzed and read out anonymously to all the groups. These groups accordingly readjusted their scores in different rounds and came out with final parameter scores after five rounds. In round five, scores given by each group nearly matched and were accepted as the most suitable by each group. This exercise brought forward the desired CFC preliminary model which could be used to give the scores for each country on the proposed new cultural dimension.

As can be seen from the above method used for suggesting a preliminary CFC model consisting of identified parameters to be used in the model and relative importance of each parameter (or weights given to each parameter), it proved to be an effective consultative process. *Delphi* technique was perfected by each focus group. As the process proceeded it became more and more clear about 'which direction study was going in terms of final accurate results'. As the process advanced, each group was very confident of being able to accurately score parameter with respect to its relative importance. Similarly, all other results from the *Delphi* sessions could be confidently recorded. The process was an important learning in terms of the inquiry of the research. Most important learning from the process was an understanding of the preliminary dimensions and variables of the construct. This 4 stage methodology provided important insights which were although qualitative in nature, but showed the way forward for a more detailed study on 'level of CFC' at multinational work places.

More importantly the current chapter lists the important parameters (or variables) which have strong bearing on the process of level of CFC. Factors like – effect of religion; effect of the attitude of the society towards foreigners; effect of the existing level of multiculturalism in society and others have been strongly highlighted in the preliminary study, which endorsed the ideas of several of the studies accounted in the literature review done in previous chapters. The methodology also provided a strong basis of developing a similar methodology for building the survey instrument for a pilot and detailed quantitative study later described in the forthcoming chapters. Interestingly, the inter country varying level CFC at multinational workplaces was distinctly clear in this chapter and is duly analyzed in later chapters. The process used in this chapter was able to provide for the preliminary results.

Country Scores based on conceptual CFC model

Average parameter weights and country wise CFC parameter scores derived in a 4 stage process above are consolidated to arrive at the desired country wise composite CFC scores. Table 7.1 gives a summary of the preliminary CFC model which emerged from the methodology described earlier in this chapter.

Table 7.1: Final Parameters and Weight Allocation

Sings	Parameters	Weights
MS	Effect of Multicultural Society: Effect of society not being substantially multicultural	10%
NR	Impact of Native's Response: Adverse response of a common native to a foreigner	20%
BC	Impact of Bureaucracy: unfavorable impact of bureaucratic setup to the comfort of a foreigner	10%
IP	Effect of Immigrant Population: Effect of non existence of substantial immigrant population in the country	5%
RM	Effect of Racism (based on skin color)	15%
GA	Government's Attitude towards Immigrants: Effect of unfavorable attitude of the state towards entry of foreigners (policy making)	10%
RT	Effect of Religious Tolerance: Effect of religious intolerance in the society	15%
EA	Impact of business owner's attitude: Adverse business owner's attitude towards foreign workers or business partners	15%

As expert groups were engaged with a bundle of information, it became more and more clear that scores can be arrived at with great conviction. Once the scores were given for each parameter, preliminary CFC scores could be established using the above preliminary CFC model. The information which was gathered for each country under study was diverse in nature but was such that it was possible to compare different countries on each of the above eight parameters.

Parameter wise CFC scores of 22 countries are tabulated in table 7.2 and the final CFC score of each country is given in the last column of the table. The final CFC score is the weighted average of scores on final eight parameters based on the appropriation suggested by expert groups. All scores are between 0 and 100. Lower scores on CFC indicates that the particular country culture is not comfortable with foreigners in different 'interaction settings'. Depending upon whether the CFC score is higher or lower, it may be possible to compare countries on how much the culture of a country tends to feel comfortable or uncomfortable with the foreigners when they encounter them in their native country in different 'interaction settings'. A 'higher CFC score' would therefore mean that the foreigners are more acceptable.

22 countries which were selected for this research study come from different continents of the world, meaning that CFC scores may give geographical idea of several regions of the world and their cultural tendency in terms of their comfort level with the presence of foreigners. Therefore, the CFC score of a country also gave an idea of a neighboring country culture even if CFC scores are not given in table 7.2 for that country.

Table 7.2: CFC Scores of 22 countries as derived from the preliminary CFC model

Country	MS[a]	NR[b]	BC[c]	IP[d]	RM[e]	GA[f]	RT[g]	EA[h]	Scores
Australia	85.0	35.0	60.0	85.0	30.0	60.0	75.0	50.0	55
Brazil	40.1	55.0	50.1	35.0	50.0	70.1	70.0	70.0	57
Canada	75.0	85.0	60.0	80.0	80.0	80.0	70.0	30.0	70
China	55.0	55.0	55.0	55.0	65.0	55.0	45.0	55.0	55
Denmark	55.0	20.0	45.0	45.0	40.0	35.0	35.0	10.0	33
France	70.0	70.0	45.0	55.0	60.0	70.0	65.0	60.0	63
Germany	75.0	50.0	40.0	60.0	55.0	40.0	75.0	70.0	59
Hungary	45.0	80.0	60.0	40.0	80.0	70.0	80.0	70.0	70
India	95.0	70.0	60.0	30.0	85.0	85.0	80.0	80.0	76
Iran	40.0	90.0	70.0	50.0	90.0	60.0	50.0	80.0	71
Italy	25.0	35.1	37.0	55.1	50.0	55.0	65.0	60.2	48
Japan	10.0	60.0	50.0	30.0	70.0	30.0	25.0	20.0	40
Kenya	30.0	50.1	35.0	30.2	70.0	69.9	74.9	70.0	57
New Zealand	85.0	50.0	70.0	80.0	40.0	80.0	75.0	45.0	62
Poland	40.0	90.0	70.0	35.0	65.0	80.0	75.0	75.0	71
Portugal	45.0	45.0	55.0	50.0	65.0	70.0	70.0	70.2	55
S. Korea	30.0	45.0	45.0	30.0	70.0	55.0	70.0	55.0	53
South Africa	70.0	30.0	60.0	60.0	30.0	60.0	70.0	60.0	52
Sweden	70.3	75.0	80.0	68.9	60.0	75.0	74.9	80.0	73
Tanzania	65.0	70.0	80.0	30.0	90.0	80.0	80.0	80.0	76
UK	75.0	65.0	55.0	60.1	50.0	60.0	74.9	80.1	66
USA	90.0	90.0	70.0	80.0	75.0	40.0	75.0	90.0	78

[a] MS   Multicultural Society
[b] NR   Native's Response
[c] BC   Bureaucracy
[d] IP   Immigrant Population

^eRM   Racism (based on skin color)
^fGA   Government's Attitude towards Immigrants
^gRT   Religious Tolerance
^hEA   Employer's attitude

Comparison of CFC scores with Hofstede's scores

In order to understand if the CFC scores arrived at based on published data has any direct correlation with the five dimensional scores of *Hofstede*; a correlation was calculated using *Pearson* correlation coefficient. Analyzing the results, it can be seen that there is no significant correlation among CFC scores and *Hofstede*'s Cultural Dimensions Scores. It indicates *Hofstede*'s topology is not predictive of the CFC scores.

Results and findings

The results and findings as described in this chapter above indicate diversity of the cultures of the world with respect to their propensity to accept foreigners in their own country and at multinational workplaces. The cultural aspect of this type otherwise, may be difficult to assess by common knowledge. This study was a first attempt to allocate scores to the countries on this dimension and will add to the existing knowledge in the areas of cross cultural management on commercial as well as non commercial situations. The results of the above kind will be helpful in making informed decisions, with respect to international strategic decisions for commercial or non commercial players.

The study of correlation of these preliminary scores with *Hofstede*'s cultural dimensions clearly showed that the concept of CFC is distinctly different from the several cultural dimensions of *Hofstede*'s and the predictions of CFC does not automatically align with the predictions of *Hofstede*'s dimensions. Therefore the concept of CFC can potentially act as a unique cultural dimension to such cross cultural studies.

It is interesting to note that there are certain countries like *US, Sweden, Poland, where* local cultures are more comfortable to foreign cultures. This list also includes *India* in the preliminary results of this chapter. However, as it appears from the comprehensive study in later chapters, there may be an inherent bias in the results related to *India* scores obtained through 'perception scaling and consultative process'. Therefore the results of this chapter are indicative only which needed to be tested more comprehensively and quantitatively.

Conclusion

This chapter has described the successful derivation of initial simple and conceptual CFC model which has been used to score different counties on CFC, based on published and secondary data. The chapter also proposed a methodology for such an exercise. More importantly, authors have proposed certain variables which are important to the phenomenon of level of CFC, which should be mastered by a cross cultural manager in international teams to manage among other things the 'level of CFC' between multicultural team members.

Suggested questions for discussion:

1) Do you think it is possible to understand a specific set of the cultural differences among nations through analyzing published data? Discuss with examples.
2) Why do many rich and developed countries too display a higher level of discomfort with foreign cultures in different kinds of interactions with them? Discuss with examples.
3) How do government policies and approaches of a country towards immigrants and foreign nationals too indicate the level of comfort or discomfort with foreigners of that particular national culture? Discuss and give examples.
4) Do you think the concept of CFC can't be explained using popular existing models like those suggested by *Hofstede* and *Trompenaars*? Discuss.
5) What kinds of different learning can be drawn from the results of the secondary data study on 'level of CFC'? Discuss.

Notes:

1. Hofstede, G. (1980). *Culture's consequences: International differences in work-related values.* Beverly Hills, CA: Sage.

2. Bose, M. (2007). *Report on racism in Polish football by the BBC.* Part of BBC Inside Sport - Poland Football Racism Special Report.

3. "Obama, Immigration Reforms." (2009). *Migration News,* 16 (3), publisher - Philip Martin, Department of Agricultural Economics, University of California, Davis, California 95616 USA

4. Foreigners enjoy living, traveling in *China.* (2004, April 10). *Xinhua News,* (p.2)

5. York, G. (2003). *Chinese Have Love-Hate Relationship with Foreigners,*

The Globe and Mail (pp. 1-14-4), Bell Globemedia Publishing Inc.

6. *Green Card Scheme – Denmark.* (n.d.). Retrieved August 01, 2012, from http://www.europeoffice.in/denmarkgreencard.html

7. Pipes, Daniel (2002). *Something is rotten in Denmark*, Retrieved July 3, 2012, from http://www.danielpipes.org

8. Multiple comments posted at *'Just Chatting'* Forum. (2012) Retrieved August 02, 2012, from www.ForeignersinDenmark.dk

9. *Foreigners In Hungary* - The "Chinese Invaders" changes in the way Hungarian perceive the Chinese community in Hungary. (2005). Retrieved Jul 15, 2012, from http://www.logoi.com/budapest/life_in_budapest/chinese_invaders_in_hungary.html

10. Hakimzadeh, Shirin (2006). *Iran: A Vast Diaspora Abroad and Millions of Refugees at Home.* Retrieved July 20, 2012, from http://www.migrationinformation.org/ profiles/ display.cfm? ID=424

11. Multiple comments posted on *Namiko's Japanese Language blog.* (2012) Retrieved August 5, 2012, form www.about.com

12. Metraux, Daniel A. (1997). "Review of To Dream of Dreams by O'Brien." *Japanese Journal of Religious Studies*, 24 (1-2), pp. 217-219.

13. Diamond, L.J. (2000). *Consolidating democracy in South Korea*, (p. 28), Based on papers of a conference held at Korea University in June 1996.

14. *The Hate is Back* (2009, July 25) Times news.

15. Naff, K.C. (2005). *Realizing a Representative Bureaucracy in South Africa: Success or Failure?* San Francisco State University, Prepared for presentation at the annual meeting of the Midwest political science association, Chicago, IL

16. *South Africa: International Religious Freedom Report* (2007), Bureau of Democracy, Human Rights, and labor, US department of State

17. *South Africa - Language, Culture, Customs and Etiquette* (n.d.). Retrieved July 28, 2012, from http://www.kwintessential.co.uk/resources/global-etiquette/south-africa-country-profile.html

18. Mukandala, R. (1999). *"Obstacles to Democratic Transition in Tanzania: An Exploratory Study on the Religious Conflict."* Paper, Unpublished.

19. Kamat, Vikas (2001). *The Diversity of India*, Retrieved July 2, 2012,

from http://www.kamat.com/indica/diversity/

20. *UN says don't blame foreigners for economic crisis.* (2009, February 24), Sydney Morning Herald

 **Online resources for this chapter, available at:**
http:/www.vijeshjain.com/books/multinational-workplaces/resources/chapter-7

8. CFC MODEL BASED ON PRIMARY DATA

This chapter describes a set of studies done to postulate a practical CFC model based on empirical primary data using suitable survey instruments. Two sets of primary data were used in these studies to devise a more versatile CFC model to understand the 'level of CFC' among members of team in multicultural multinational workplaces. A first set of data is a pilot data collected from several countries with the help of research collaborators in these individual countries. Using the survey instrument as discussed in an earlier chapter, administered online in different local languages as well as in *English*, data collected was tested for validity, reliability and suitability. At the same time validity and suitability of the questionnaire itself were also tested in this primary study. Latent variables emerged from exploratory factor analysis were analyzed and discussed for their nature and behavior to arrive at a more versatile CFC model suitable for further fine tuning by a second set of data (a larger set of respondent data).

This part of the chapter describes the attempts to analyze cross cultural differences among nations related to 'level of CFC' in multinational firms, using pilot sample survey data based on a field study of employee behavior in multinational firms based in different nations. Therefore, this section describes the methodology and results of a pilot study done to see CFC differences as well as subsequently conducting a full scale comprehensive cross cultural comparison through a larger sample data. The pilot study was done on a set of countries / regions of the world through convenience sampling using 'CFC questionnaire' administered online. The analysis of the data based on the CFC questionnaire scales indicated visible differences among nations / regions on their comfort level with foreign cultures when studied at MNE workplaces. The process of developing the survey instrument was discussed in an earlier chapter.

The survey questionnaire development was motivated and helped by the experience of the preliminary conceptual study as discussed in the previous chapter. In the study discussed in previous chapter, it was shown what methods were adopted to undertake a preliminary exploratory conceptual study based on secondary data to determine a simple framework for CFC model which can be used to score countries on level of CFC. In this part of the study a CFC model was devised using the primary data which was the respondent data collected from several countries using online questionnaires as already discussed. For these two approaches had been adopted.

In the first approach a pilot study was done to investigate a set of countries based on a scientifically designed framework using survey instrument and involving a moderate size of the sample. In the second approach, a more detailed analysis was carried out using a larger survey data collected from a smaller number of countries, based on more accurate survey instrument. It should be noted that pilot study was only a precursor to a detailed survey based quantitative study. In the first part of the chapter authors have discussed the methodology adopted in the pilot survey data based study.

The methodology used

For this part of the study, the authors utilized a three-part methodology to understand 'level of CFC' in multinational companies. This methodology consisted of-

1. Collection of data using the online survey instrument (already discussed in an earlier chapter)
2. Exploratory factor analysis on a data set utilized for pilot study with IBM SPSS Statistics Base
3. The study of the nature and behavior of latent variables emerged from the second step using respondent data

The sample size was 361 from 9 countries, 179 of whom were men and 182 were women, each working for global companies having operations in different countries. All respondents who met the inclusion criteria of the study were working for multinational firms in their respective countries of residence. The inclusion criteria for the study were - all respondents must be well educated, exposed to a multicultural working environment in a multi country organization, and routinely working and interacting with colleagues with origins from several countries.

Sources and types of data

The data were collected on a global platform with the help of collaborator in different countries. A total of 15 research collaborators helped in collecting data online. It may be noted that data collection was uneven from different countries since authors and the collaborators virtually had no control on how many respondents undertake the survey instrument. Finally valid data was available from 9 counties in the pilot study. A total of 361 valid responses from 9 countries was selected for the pilot study. The development of survey instruments and questions covered in the same are already discussed an earlier chapter. These responses were part of the total of 450 responses authors and research collaborators could gather for pilot study from more than 15 countries.

Baseline characteristics

A number of socio- demographic characteristics of respondents who participated were collected. More specifically, following were recorded:

1. Sex & Age of the respondents

2. Educational level

3. Residence status in their country of stay

4. Their relative income level

Research methods and techniques used

As already discussed authors utilized a three-part methodology to understand level of CFC in multinational companies, first two of which consisted of-

1) Survey instrument development,

2) Exploratory factor analysis on dataset 1 with IBM SPSS Statistics Base.

Since authors used a sample size of 361 the same was suitable for the method of pilot research. EFA was conducted on respondent data from 361 respondents using IBM SPSS Statistics Base, after entering survey data. As already discussed a set of observed variables or questions of the questionnaire was arrived at with the help of 200 volunteers using *the Delphi technique*. The volunteers consisted of cross cultural experts and students of cross cultural courses. The volunteers were grouped in 10 groups. The *Delphi* sessions were performed in 2 stages. The volunteers were apprised of the results of a preliminary model of CFC arrived at as explained in an earlier chapter. The literature review related to the study was also shared with them.

In the next step the above model was given to a random sample of 450 MNE employees from more than 15 countries, in the form of an online questionnaire. Using EFA (exploratory factor analysis), latent variables were identified and categorized. The method for the data collection was 'filling out an online questionnaire', using the above CFC questionnaire, which is supposed to have fully met the requirements of the current study and consisted of the questions of 'assessment of the level of comfort of the local cultures with foreign cultures at MNE work places and descriptive characteristics. The *Likert* type 'five point scale' was used to answer all questions. The five different scales were represented with the following answers: Strongly Agree, Agree, Neutral, Disagree and Strongly Disagree. The process of filling out the questionnaires usually took between 15 and 30 minutes each. The results of the questionnaire survey were entered into IBM SPSS Statistics Base software for exploratory factor analysis to identify and test latent variables or CFC scales which could form part of the survey based CFC model. This model was further used to score countries on CFC scales.

Identification of latent variables using exploratory factor analysis

The survey data was entered into the IBM SPSS Statistics Base and exploratory factor analysis provided 11 factors. The factor analysis was used to obtain a CFC model. The suitability, reliability and validity of the data for carrying out such analysis are discussed later. Each factor that emerged was interpreted based on the questions that had load value > 0.3. Evaluation of the internal consistency of the observed variables of the CFC questionnaire was carried out by calculating the *Standardized Cronbach Alpha* coefficient and calculating reliability estimates. The model which emerged from this exercise is given in table 8.1.

Table 8.1: CFC model as obtained from Delphi sessions and Exploratory Factor Analysis (EFA)

PART 1 (General Sub - scales)	Full Question
S1: Seeing Benefits in Cross Cultures	
S1.1: Cross cultural interaction should be encouraged	Interacting with people from different countries should be encouraged because it will help us improve our own values and

	beliefs
S1.2: Important to learn other cultures	I think it is important to learn more about other cultures
S1.3: Immigrants add value	I consider foreign immigration as a value added our country's economy
S1.4: Like to know differences to build friendship	Knowing how a person differs from me may help me build our friendship
S1.5: like to see foreigners coming to my country	I would like seeing people from other countries come to my country
S1.6: I find other cultures are similar to us	If I get to know people from other countries and other cultures, I learn that we are more alike than different
S1.7: Learn from other cultures	I always put efforts to learn from other cultures in one way or another

S2: Willingness to Socialize with foreigners

S2.1: Like to visit a foreigner	If I was invited by a foreigner to his house, I will surely follow the invitation
S2.2: Good feeling to meet a foreigner	I am more likely to feel good to visit a foreigner
S2.3: New learning from visiting a foreigner	If I were invited by a foreigner to visit, it is likely to be a new learning experience for me
S2.4: Enjoy foreign food	I enjoy eating food of the types originating overseas/from other countries
S2.5: Fun to learn about foreigners	Getting to know people from another culture is generally fun for me
S2.6: Comfortable with foreigners	I feel comfortable being around foreigners

S3: Agreeing to equal status to world cultures

S3.1: Nothing like my culture represent more values and ethics	I do not think my country's dominant cultures represent more values and ethics than many other cultures of the world
S3.2: My culture does not need better recognition	I do not think of the need for my culture getting better recognition in the world of today to solve many of the problems being faced by the humanity
S3.3: All cultures have the same status	I do not think there are cultures in the world which may be more superior or more refined

than others

S3.4: Not like Immigrants getting better salary than us	I do not think Foreigners living and working in our country are being offered better salaries and more respect than our own people

S4: Level of Personal Comfort

S4.1: No problem with a foreign boss	I would be comfortable with a colleague from a different culture in a superior position to me
S4.2: No problem with a foreign junior	I would be comfortable with a colleague from a different culture in an inferior position to me
S4.3: No problem with a foreign roommate	I would be comfortable with a roommate from another culture
S4.4: Friends must agree with me	I see it's important for me that friends agree with me on most issues
S4.5: No problem with a homosexual	I have no issues if someone I know has a homosexual orientation

S5: Willingness to Explore Foreign Cultures

S5.1: Desire to travel abroad	Not like I have no desire to travel abroad
S5.2: I will be welcome abroad	Not like I have no desire to travel abroad because I would feel insecure and unwelcome amongst people from a different culture
S5.3: Willing to venture into foreign cultures	Not like I may never want to move to a new country, even if I have better prospects mainly due to the fact that I am unwilling to venture into foreign cultures
S5.4: Like to have a vacation abroad	If I won a free vacation, I would rather spend it in a different country where I am likely to learn about new cultures and ways of life

S6: Positive views about Globalization

S6.1: No need to stop globalization	I do not think Something should be done to stop such damage
S6.2: No cultural damage by globalization	Globalization of cultures have not damaged my cultural, economic and religious traditions in many ways
S6.3: Immigrants do not	I do not think Foreigners living and working

steal jobs	in our country are stealing away the benefits and privileges from their rightful owners
S6.4: New ideas coming due to globalization	Globalization has resulted in new ideas and positive cultural influences coming into your country from other countries
S6.5: Can't stop globalization	Globalization of cultures will happen anyway and cannot be stopped

S7: Favorable impact of Religion

S7.1: Religion not part of daily life	I do not think religion is a part of my daily life
S7.2: No existence of a supernatural power	I do not think there exists a supernatural power which may monitor my activities and perhaps influence me in any way
S7.3: Religious Society	My native society (read country) is religious
S7.4: Curious to know other religious thoughts	I was curious to know more about his/her religious beliefs
S7.5: No Global problems due to religious beliefs	I do not think there are problems in the modern world which relates to religious beliefs

S8: Positive attitude of society towards foreigners

S8.1: Problem may not increase with foreigners	The probability of being branded as accused would not increase if the innocent persons also happen to be foreigners
S8.2: No Victimization of foreigners based on their religious beliefs	I have never witnessed incidents involving a person of foreign origin persecuted or victimized for his foreign religious belief in my society
S8.3: Unrelated person never getting randomly targeted	There are no insecurities related to the sudden turn of events which may result in an unrelated person getting targeted by the society (where I live in) at large
S8.4: Rational Society for foreigners	The society (I live in) remains rational in a situation of major crisis involving those which may apparently look like to have been created by certain groups or persons of certain foreign origin or race
S8.5: Irrational behavior of victims blaming a foreigner	In a situation of certain crisis have you witnessed victims behaving irrationally accusing a certain group of persons based on

their nationality or race?

S8.6: Branded accused without proof	Do you think there is a possibility of innocent persons being branded as accused without enough proof in your society

S9: How liberal is the society?

S9.1: Belief in the theory of evolution	I believe in the theory of evolution
S9.2: No encounter with persons preaching their religious beliefs	I have never come across some persons preaching me on his religious orientation

S10: Willingness to use foreign products

S10.1: Watch foreign movies	I often watch foreign movies because they are windows to different cultures and their ways of life
S10.2: Buy foreign clothing	I like to buy foreign clothing brands because I want to keep up with the global trends in fashion
S10.3: Listen to foreign music	I often listen to foreign music for being different and broadening my world view

S11: Ease of understanding

S11.1: No problem to understand foreigners	When dealing with persons of foreign origin I never had difficulty in understanding his or her point of view
S11.2: No Repulsion with people of other religion	It is not difficult for me to feel close to people who have a different religion from mine
S11.3: No difficulty in understanding of diverse world cultures	I never have any difficulty in understanding of diverse world cultures

---

PART 2: (Conditional Sub - scales)

ST1: Stereotype- Higher Income Group Views

ST1.1: Enterprising Below Income	Below average income persons are generally enterprising enough to look forward to a bright rich future
ST1.2: Below income as Loyal Employees	Below average income persons can generally be trusted as loyal employees
ST1.3: Below income as	Below average income persons can generally be trusted to work given to them for

Trustworthy	monetary rewards

ST2: Stereotype- Lower Income Group Views

ST2.1: Caring higher income	Above average income persons care about the lower income group
ST2.2: Reliable higher income	Above average income persons can generally be relied on
ST2.3: Helpful higher income	Above average income persons may be willing to help highly needy lower income group persons with money or other resources

ST3: Stereotype-Men's Views

ST3.1: More Chores for women	Women should do more house chores than men
ST3.2: Women more talkative	Women are more talkative and cannot keep an important family secret for long
ST3.3: Women likes to be with women	Women generally like the company of females more than males

ST4: Stereotype- Women's Views

ST4.1: Caring Men	Men generally care enough for the emotions of women
ST4.2: Loving Men	Men generally love the way women want them to be
ST4.3: Respecting Men	Men normally respect women and tend to give the first right of way

ST5: Stereotype- Situational Discrimination

Have you ever had a problem with a foreigner? If yes answer the following questions

ST5.1: No Problem with countrymen	The problem may not have occurred if the person happened to be a fellow countryman
ST5.2: Different behavior with countrymen	I would have behaved differently if the person would have been a fellow countryman
ST5.3: Foreigner should be more careful	The person should have been more careful in dealing with me, because of his/her foreign origin while being in my country
ST5.4: Problem related to his origin	The peculiar behavior of the person was related to his/her cultural origin
ST5.5: Behavior was expected due to his origin	His/her behavior was on expected lines in keeping with his/her specific foreign origin

PART 3: (Demographic Questions - General)	
Country of Residence	Present Country of Residence
Region	Geographical Region
City of Residence	Present City of Residence
Age	Age
Residential Status	Residential Status
Education Level	Education Level
Income Group	Income Group

Reliability and validity assessment of the questionnaire

Validity: Initially, the questionnaire, immediately after the design, was submitted to 20 respondents to determine whether the questions were clear, understandable, and in a logical order (face validity). The construct validity of the questionnaire was tested using the appropriate statistical technique in order to determine the structure of the questionnaire. The criterion validity of the questionnaire was not checked, as a gold standard tool for assessment of the level of comfort, of local cultures with foreign cultures in multinational Companies has not been proposed yet.

Reliability: Finally, the internal consistency and the repeatability of each question derived from the construct validity of the questionnaire were tested using the appropriate statistical tests. In particular, 50 respondents were used in order to assess the repeatability. These respondents completed the questionnaire two times. Between the two measurements there was a period of three to four days. The suitability of the data for carrying out such analysis was tested by using the *Bartlett Sphericity Test* and the *Kaiser-Meyer-Olkin (KMO) statistic test* that evaluates the degree of correlation among the questions included in the questionnaire.

Exploratory factor analysis (EFA)

Statistically significant results of the *Sphericity* test indicated that the variance- covariance matrix of the initial questions of the questionnaire is not diagonal (i.e., variables are correlated with each other). Also, values of KMO> 0.8 indicated a fairly high correlation and therefore, factor analysis is meaningful. The method of 'Maximum likelihood' was used for assessment / extraction of the main factors[1]. *The criterion of Kaiser (Eigenvalue > 1)* was used to determine the number of factors derived from the factor analysis. An orthogonal rotation (in this case *Varimax*) was used to improve the explanatory ability of the factors. Each factor that emerged was interpreted based on the questions that had load value > 0.3.

Evaluation of the internal consistency of the observed variables of the CFC questionnaire was carried out by calculating the *Standardized Cronbach Alpha* coefficient and calculating reliability estimates. *Cronbach* coefficient ranges from 0 - 1. Large *Cronbach Alpha* values indicate a high consistency of the questions of which the sub-scale is consisted. The '*Cronbach Alpha* if item deleted' index was used to identify the questions that reduced the internal consistency of the questionnaire and therefore had to be excluded. The repeatability of questionnaire was evaluated by using *McDonald Omega* which is a measure of generalizablity of the test questions or observed variables. It varies between 0 to 1. Omega can be interpreted as the square of the correlation between the scale score and the latent variable common to all the indicators in the infinite universe of indicators of which the scale indicators are a subset[2]. The greatest lower bound was calculated for reliability testing. The greatest lower bound (glb) to reliability represents the smallest reliability possible given observed covariance matrix under the restriction that the sum of error variances is maximized for errors that correlate with other variables[3].

All statistical analysis was carried out using IBM SPSS Statistics Base Software. The method used for the pilot study was suitable for a gross sample size of 450 and a net sample size of 361. Most of the statistical results are in congruence with each other and the pilot CFC model which emerged was found to be suitable for a study of this type. However, it was felt that a confirmatory factor analysis (CFA) was required for a more comprehensive study of this type to further fine tune the CFC model. CFA was not done in this pilot study due to lesser sample size. Reliability and validity of the sample data and the questionnaire was duly tested, and results of such tests have been favorable.

The data was found to be reliable and questionnaire also was suitable for this study. It is interesting to note that many of the emerged latent variables (using EFA) were in line with the theoretical discussions explained in an earlier chapter. Of special mention are latest variables like–

1) Effect of religion,
2) Effect of society's attitude,
3) Views about globalization and others.

These variables have been mentioned in various cross cultural studies as discussed in earlier chapters. Nevertheless, there have emerged another set of latent variables in this pilot study which were not directly mentioned in other studies. Some of these factors are:

1) Willingness to explore foreign cultures,
2) Personal ease with foreigners,
3) Seeing benefit from cross cultural interaction.

Each of these latent variables was supported by a suitable set of observed variables which made the variable results more useful for this study. Therefore the emerged questionnaire structure could be used as a basis for a comprehensive quantitative study on 'level of CFC' as is discussed later in this chapter.

A detailed analysis of latent variables of the CFC model was subsequently done and interpretation was drawn about the behavior of the emerged latent variables. These latent variables which were studied are:

Seeing the benefits in cross cultural engagements: There is a section of society which sees more or less the benefits in cross cultural engagement. As it seems to indicate from the data related to above latent variable (CFC scale), *India* and *Italy* appear to see much lesser benefit in engagements with foreign cultures when compared with other countries under study. Interestingly, both countries have adverse views about the benefits of inbound immigration in their countries. On the other side, *Sweden* seems to see the most benefit in such engagements. Even in the case of *Sweden*, responses show most adverse view about the benefits of inbound immigration to *Sweden*. *Italy* show most adverse view about immigration among all countries.

A willingness to socialize with foreigners: This analysis was based on the postulation that there can be differences between several sections of a society where some persons may have comparatively more willingness than others to socialize with alien cultures. The extent of society having less or more desire to socialize may vary from country to country. As could be seen from the mean of the responses on this CFC scale in this part of analysis, it seems that *China* and *India* desire least to socialize with foreigners when compared with other countries under study. On the other extreme, *Portugal* & *Kenya* seem to desire more than others to socialize with foreigners. Willingness to visit a foreigner seems to be least in case of *India*. As also *India* responses showed, it is comparatively less comfortable with foreigners when asked a direct question on comfort.

Agreeing to equal status to world cultures: This analysis was based on the postulation that societies globally may differ on their level of comfort with foreign cultures due to the fact that they are more patriotic than others and this patriotism may possibly make them less comfortable with foreign cultures. As indicated by this analysis, *India* followed by *Italy* seemed to get more influenced by the feelings of patriotism than other countries which may make them lesser comfortable than other countries with foreign cultures. *China* was also not far behind. *Sweden* seemed to be least influenced. *Indian* seemed to be having a strong view that its own culture represents more values and ethics than other cultures of the world.

Level of personal comfort: There can be differences among different cultures around the world based on the personal comfort attributes which may have an impact on the variation of the comfort level of these cultures with foreign cultures. This attribute of personal comfort was also analyzed. As is indicated by this analysis, *India* seemed to have lesser personal comfort when compared with other countries of the study. *Sweden* appeared to be having most personal comfort with foreign cultures. Most adverse feelings in *India* related to personal comfort with homosexuals. Although this may not fully translate into personal comfort with foreigners, this feeling does indicate personal comfort with perceived aliens. Interestingly, *Sweden* did not represent major repulsion with homosexuality or homosexuals as also their comfort level with foreigners. Among the boss, a junior and a roommate, *Indian* responses showed least comfort with a foreign roommate.

Willingness to explore foreign cultures: Desire to explore foreign cultures may indicate a certain comfort level of local cultures with foreign cultures owing to the effect of personal motivation and interests. Such variation in the desire to explore foreign cultures is likely to have an impact on the overall comfort level of local cultures with alien cultures. This analysis gave indication to such variations. As appeared from this analysis, *India* seemed to have a lesser desire than others, to explore foreign cultures. Therefore, it may be possible that this may contribute to *India*'s lesser comfort with foreign cultures on this dimension. On the other side *Sweden* seemed to show most desire to explore foreign cultures. There is a stark difference in willingness to travel abroad among *India* responses when compared with responses from *Sweden*.

Positive views about globalization: In a fast developing globalized world where economic, technological, financial and even political integration is taking place on a fast paced level, there can be different views about this process of globalization. These views may also indicate differences in level of comfort, of the local cultures with foreign cultures. This aspect of cultural reality was analyzed. As can be inferred from visual analysis of respondent data using mean score value of each question under this latent variable, *India* seemed to have comparatively more adverse views about globalization as compared to other countries being studied. Most favorable views about globalization seemed to have emerged from *US* followed by *Italy*, *China* and other western countries. However, on the question of the need to stop globalization, *Kenya* seemed to have the most adverse views and was in great contrast to other countries. *Indian* views were not far behind on this issue.

The favorable impact of religion: It may be possible that a highly religious society may indicate a lesser comfort level with foreign cultures, particularly those practicing different religions than local cultures and in the views of certain authors, religion itself may work as a religious cultural system vary with geographical location on the planet[4]. This variation on its effect on comfort was indicated in the analysis of the associated questions under this latent variable through visual analysis of the mean scores of the questions. It appeared from above analysis that *Kenya* and *India* seemed to be more religious societies than others. However *Italy* followed by *China* appeared to be less religious. *Kenya* indicated most that religion plays an important role in their daily life. *India* believed most in the existence of a super-natural power. *Italians* saw minimum role for religion in their daily life.

The positive attitude of society towards foreigners: If a society has a tendency of adverse attitude towards unrelated persons and persons of foreign origin, it may be possible that they may show signs of discomfort with foreign cultures. Analysis studied this variation about the nature of the societies of the countries studied. As it seemed from the above analysis, *Italy* seemed to be having most tendency of having most adverse attitude towards unrelated or persons of foreign origin. Similarly *Sweden*, *Brazil* and *US* also show such tendencies. *Portugal* and *Kenya* fairs best in this respect where it appears society's behavior is more rational in such matters.

Willingness to use foreign goods and services: A society, most using foreign goods and services may be showing signs of more comfort with foreign cultures than others. Here authors analyzed this aspect. As it may seem from this analysis, *Sweden* seemed to use lesser foreign products than others. At the same time, *Brazil* seemed to be the most interested to use foreign products. This may indicate more comfort of *Brazil* with foreign cultures than others. However, it may be interesting to note that nature of the products used varied strongly among countries. *Sweden* was the least user of foreign clothing, while *India* and *China* seemed to be least interested in listening foreign music. Interestingly, *China* seemed to be most interested to watch foreign movies. *Brazil* seemed to be most interested to listen to foreign music.

Ease of understanding of foreign cultures Societies: Having ease of understanding of other cultures is likely to show more signs of comfort with foreign cultures than others. This variation was also analyzed. As it appears, *Portugal* seemed to be feeling most easy to understand foreign cultures followed by *Kenya*, *Italy*, *Brazil* and *UK*. While most of the other countries do not feel so easy, *India* appeared to be having least ease to understand foreign cultures.

Stereotypes among income groups

Higher stereotype among income groups is indicative of the tendency of the society to develop stereotype which may also translate into their interactions with foreigners. Societal fault lines between income groups also seem to indicate similar phenomenon on a higher scale. Comparisons of the means of the responses (dependent variables) to questions related to this attribute against independent variables, namely regions, as calculated using the SPSS 20 program was analyzed. As could be analyzed from the comparison, showing means of the different questions data related to the views of lower income groups in various regions studied, there appeared to be societal fault lines among low income groups in *the US* and *European* Countries with higher stereotype among low income groups. Among Swedish low income groups stereotype was found to be higher. Fault lines between income groups are much less in case of *India, Kenya, Brazil* and *China* and as such the stereotype is moderate.

Stereotypes among genders

As viewed, societal fault lines are strong in almost all countries studied except in the *UK*.

There are visible variations between males and female stereotypes among different countries, while in females in *Brazil*, and *US* have stronger stereotypes, males in *Portugal* seems to have stronger stereotype about males.

Situational discrimination

There were around 152 respondents who have had a behavioral problem or confrontation with a foreigner in their own countries. The analysis studied, the mean scores of certain questions asked to these respondents about their reactions to foreigners in such situation. As could be seen in the above comparison, behavioral discomfort with a foreigner, in such a situation, appeared to be starker in the case of *Portugal* and *Kenya*. *US* fared better than others on this attribute with least behavioral problem in such a situation. In case of *Kenya* & *Portugal* also above data indicated a behavioral problem with foreigners.

Ranking of countries on their overall comfort level scores

Based on the above observations a ranking of the countries studied could be done. We calculated the overall mean on CFC based on all sub scales. The final notional overall ranking of the countries based on their overall comfort level as analyzed by the pilot study above appears to be as in table 8.2. As can be seen from the table 8.2, there is lesser conflict in the overall national ranks calculated based on overall rank totals and overall mean scores. However, in case of *the US* and *China* there is a significant conflict of ranking based on two methods.

Table 8.2: Overall national ranks (based on rank totals and overall mean)

Name of the country	Rank 1	Rank 2
Brazil	5	6
China	6	2.5
India	9	9
Italy	8	8
Kenya	7	7
Portugal	4	5
Sweden	2	1
UK	3	4
USA	1	2.5

The data analysis clearly showed through the pilot study that there are differences of level of comfort with foreign cultures from country to country. However, these differences were to be tested to confirm the significance of these differences which would require a comprehensive large scale study.

In the next part of this chapter, we have discussed the analysis of the large scale study of three countries and can see if there are significant differences among countries in final CFC scores. Ranks of many counties are in line with the ranks as emerging in the preliminary conceptual study as described in the previous chapter. It is interesting to note from the above pilot results that rank of *India* on level of CFC has slipped several steps when compared with the results of preliminary conceptual simple study. A possible reason for this difference is the inherent bias of the volunteers in the preliminary qualitative study. It is also interesting to note that the estimation of the country ranks based on the 2 pronged approaches gave a somewhat similar picture of country ranking. It supports the pilot research methodology used.

CFC model based on comprehensive three country study

All the initial results obtained in the earlier part of this chapter have been consolidated to fine tune the CFC model which is more robust, scalable and usable to score different cultures of the world on CFC. Therefore, use of a larger sample base of three countries using inter country study has been described in this chapter to have a micro level look at the phenomenon of 'Level of CFC' in this chapter. Using SPSS Amos, a confirmatory analysis based on structural equation modeling had been used to see error terms in the newly created CFC model using EFA. Further, using the new model, the impact of different control variables including 'country' on new CFC scales had been studied in depth, using a 2 way ANOVA. It should be noted that the authors had tested the survey instrument as well as data for validity and reliability and inferences could be made using this data on the behavior of specific cultural dimensions which forms part of the overall level of CFC. In this part of the chapter a discussion is also made of the control variables which were identified which should logically impact the different cultural dimensions based on valid data collected from eligible respondents. Thereafter CFC models were used, to verify the effect of 'country and other control variables' on these dimensions of an entire country cross cultural comparison. On the national level cross cultural comparison, authors similarly analyzed the effects of city wise responses (as described in the last part of this chapter) to see whether the level of intercultural comfort varied city wise and due to other control variables. The authors also proposed CFC scores of several countries included in the study in this book, for a quick comparison of our main construct on a global level.

The survey instrument was further fine tuned using CFA in this part of the study. As discussed earlier in the chapter, it was seen how authors used a combination of 'perception scaling and consultative process' coupled with EFA to identify both the observed and latent variables which could explain the phenomenon of level of comfort with foreign cultures in multinational firms. And how these frameworks were validated and tested for reliability using survey instrument. In this part authors attempted to further refine the survey instrument and carry out a confirmatory factor analysis using a larger sample size and using structural equation modeling (using IBM SPSS AMOS).

Research design and modeling

A survey instrument derived in the earlier part was further applied to a much larger sample of three countries. The latent variables were again identified and CFC model was fine tuned using CFA (more specifically structural equation modeling). To investigate whether different latent variables derived from observed variables, have a direct relationship with intercultural comfort, control variables were identified and their impact on each CFC scale (latent variables) was statistically tested using 2 Ways ANOVA.

Sources and types of data

The respondents from several countries were invited to take the online survey tool. The respondents were working adults having worked with cross cultural teams on international projects in multinational companies. The eligible respondents in different countries were identified and invited to take the survey instrument with the help of research collaborators in different countries. A total of valid 995 respondents from more than 10 countries took the online survey. The CFC model was tested and refined on this data from 995 respondents. However, for the cross cultural comparison of CFC scale among countries a total data of 835 valid responses was selected from three countries – namely *India*, *Portugal* and *Italy*. The elimination of other countries for cross cultural comparison was done due to small sample size of the respondents from other countries.

Primary sources of data

Data was collected using CFC questionnaire obtained from focus groups and walk-through assessments of intercultural group comfort dynamics as discussed in the earlier part of the chapter and using *the Delphi technique* to identify all gamut of observed variables in which authors took the cross cultural perspective as explained in detail in the earlier section of this chapter.

The methodology used for data analysis

For this research, the authors utilized a four-part methodology to understand level of CFC in multinational firms. This methodology consisted of:

1. Survey instrument development (using *the Delphi technique* and walk through assessment of questions included in the questionnaire based on the literature review)

2. Exploratory factor analysis on dataset 1 with IBM SPSS Statistics Base

3. Confirmatory factor analysis (CFA) and structural equation modeling (SEM) on dataset 2 (i.e., confirming correlations and inferred causal relationships among factors)

4. Analysis of CFC scales emerged from above steps for their behavior under control variables like country, gender, educational levels, age group, and income group.

Using IBM SPSS Statistics Base, authors entered the results from the online surveys and used descriptive statistics to identify outliers that may result from possible data entry errors. Thereafter, the authors split the survey data into two parts and ran an exploratory factor analysis on one dataset to determine the underlying factor structures (in other words, the authors explored which observed variables were associated with each latent variable or construct, such as 'personal comfort with foreign cultures')

Reliability and validity testing of the CFC model

Finally, using the results of EFA, authors leveraged IBM SPSS Amos' interface to run a CFA, using the second data set to examine the reliability and validity of the measurement model without identifying the directional relationship among the factors (i.e., where all factors are related, graphically depicted with double-headed arrows). The authors then drew on the hypothesized model and examined the underlying directional relationships among CFC scales or latent variables. In figure 8.1, these relationships are connected with single-headed arrows.

Since the fit indices authors obtained were acceptable, it was known authors had identified a model that fit the survey based data (i.e., both the comparative fit index (CFI) and the *Tucker-Lewis index* (TLI) were close to .95, and the root mean square error of approximation (RMSEA) was smaller than .08).

This model allowed authors to graphically view the inferred causal relationships between different dimensions (latent variables) of intercultural comfort (an exogenous dependable variable). The pictorial graph in Figure 8.1 was generated using IBM SPSS Amos and illustrates the findings of CFA. The squares represent the questions, or items, asked during the survey phase (e.g., question S1.1 asked 'Cross cultural interaction should be encouraged') and are also known as observed variables. The ovals represent the latent (non-observed) variables, also described as constructs or dimensions. It is important to note that the ovals are not actual variables. Rather, they are factors defined by the observed variables (rectangles). For the purpose of simplicity, error measurement terms are not shown.

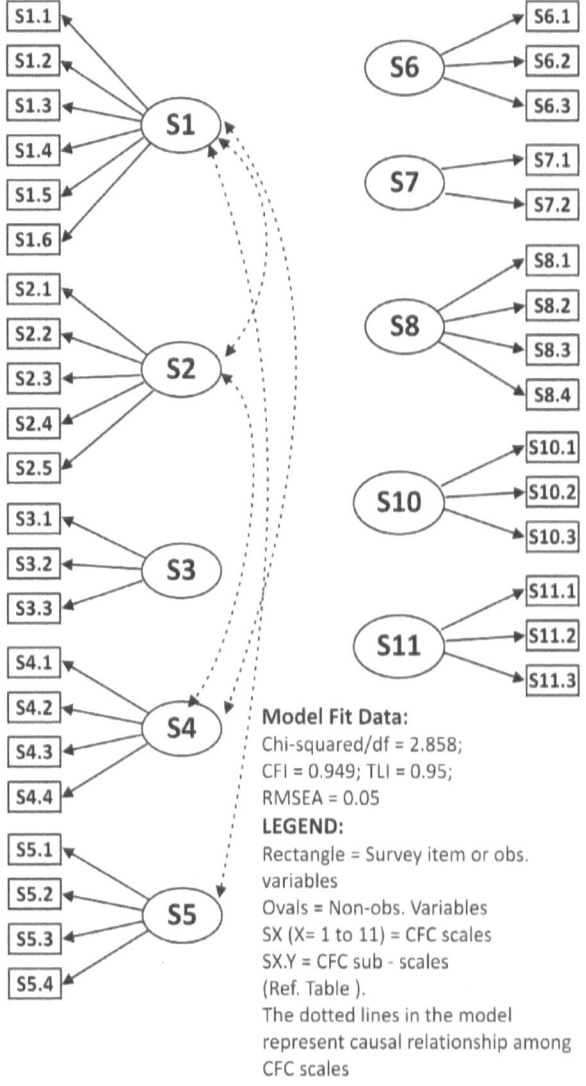

Model Fit Data:
Chi-squared/df = 2.858;
CFI = 0.949; TLI = 0.95;
RMSEA = 0.05
LEGEND:
Rectangle = Survey item or obs. variables
Ovals = Non-obs. Variables
SX (X= 1 to 11) = CFC scales
SX.Y = CFC sub - scales
(Ref. Table).
The dotted lines in the model represent causal relationship among CFC scales

Figure 8.1: SEM as used for CFA for finding refined CFC model

Final CFC model

A final CFC model which was used for cross cultural comparison of three countries and which emerged from the above 3 stage methodology looked like the one given in table 8.3 below.

Table 8.3: CFC model after SEM

PART 1 (General Sub - scales)	Full Question
S1: Seeing the benefits in cross cultural interactions	
S1.1: Cross cultural interaction should be encouraged	Interacting with people from different countries should be encouraged because it will help us improve our own values and beliefs
S1.2: Important to learn other cultures	I think it is important to learn more about other cultures
S1.3: Immigrants add value	I consider foreign immigration as a value added our country's economy
S1.4: Like to know differences to build friendship	Knowing how a person differs from me may help me build our friendship
S1.5: like to see foreigners coming to my country	I would like seeing people from other countries come to my country
S1.6: I find other cultures are similar to us	If I get to know people from other countries and other cultures, I learn that we are more alike than different
S2: Willingness to socialize with foreigners	
S2.1: Like to visit a foreigner	If I was invited by a foreigner to his house, I will surely follow the invitation
S2.2: Good feeling to meet a foreigner	I am more likely to feel good to visit a foreigner
S2.3: New learning from visiting a foreigner	If I were invited by a foreigner to visit, it is likely to be a new learning experience for me

S2.5: Fun to learn about foreigners	Getting to know people from another culture is generally fun for me
S2.6: Comfortable with foreigners	I feel comfortable being around foreigners

S3: Agreeing to the equal status to several world cultures

S3.1: Nothing like my culture represent more values and ethics	I do not think my country's dominant cultures represent more values and ethics than many other cultures of the world
S3.2: My culture does not need better recognition	I do not think of the need for my culture getting better recognition in the world of today to solve many of the problems being faced by the humanity
S3.3: All cultures have the same status	I do not think there are cultures in the world which may be more superior or more refined than others

S4: Level of personal comfort

S4.1: No problem with a foreign boss	I would be comfortable with a colleague from a different culture in a superior position to me
S4.2: No problem with a foreign junior	I would be comfortable with a colleague from a different culture in an inferior position to me
S4.3: No problem with a foreign roommate	I would be comfortable with a roommate from another culture
S4.5: No problem with a homosexual	I have no issues if someone I know has a homosexual orientation

S5: Willingness to explore foreign cultures

S5.1: Desire to travel abroad	Not like I have no desire to travel abroad
S5.2: I will be welcome abroad	Not like I have no desire to travel abroad because I would feel insecure and unwelcome amongst people from a

142

	different culture
S5.3: Willing to venture into foreign cultures	Not like I may never want to move to a new country, even if I have better prospects mainly due to the fact that I am unwilling to venture into foreign cultures
S5.4: Like to have a vacation abroad	If I won a free vacation, I would rather spend it in a different country where I am likely to learn about new cultures and ways of life

S6: Positive views about globalization

S6.1: No need to stop globalization	I do not think Something should be done to stop such damage
S6.2: No cultural damage by globalization	Globalization of cultures have not damaged my cultural, economic and religious traditions in many ways
S6.3: Immigrants do not steal jobs	I do not think Foreigners living and working in our country are stealing away the benefits and privileges from their rightful owners

S7: Favorable impact of religion

S7.1: Religion not part of daily life	I do not think religion is a part of my daily life
S7.2: No existence of a supernatural power	I do not think there exists a supernatural power which may monitor my activities and perhaps influence me in any way

S8: Positive attitude of society towards foreigners

S8.1: Problem may not increase with foreigners	The probability of being branded as accused would not increase if the innocent persons also happen to be foreigners
S8.2: No Victimization of foreigners based on their	I have never witnessed incidents involving a person of foreign origin

religious beliefs	persecuted or victimized for his foreign religious belief in my society
S8.3: Unrelated person never getting randomly targeted	There are no insecurities related to the sudden turn of events which may result in an unrelated person getting targeted by the society (where I live in) at large
S8.4: Rational Society for foreigners	The society (I live in) remains rational in a situation of major crisis involving those which may apparently look like to have been created by certain groups or persons of certain foreign origin or race
S9: How liberal is the society?	
S9.1: Belief in the theory of evolution	I believe in the theory of evolution
S9.2: No encounter with persons preaching their religious beliefs	I have never come across some persons preaching me on his religious orientation
S10: Willingness to Use Foreign Products	
S10.1: Watch foreign movies	I often watch foreign movies because they are windows to different cultures and their ways of life
S10.2: Buy foreign clothing	I like to buy foreign clothing brands because I want to keep up with the global trends in fashion
S10.3: Listen to foreign music	I often listen to foreign music for being different and broadening my world view
S11: Ease of understanding	
S11.1: No problem to understand foreigners	When dealing with persons of foreign origin I never had difficulty in understanding his or her point of view
S11.2: No Repulsion with people of other religion	It is not difficult for me to feel close to people who have a different religion from mine

S11.3: No difficulty in understanding of diverse world cultures	I never have any difficulty in understanding of diverse world cultures

Identification of control variables

Using the demographic information and discussions based on literature review as described above, authors identified control variables. Thus genders, income group, education level, age group, country of origin and city of residence were identified as control variables for several variables and scales identified in the questionnaire. Based on these control variables, respondent data were analyzed and interpretations were made as described in the following section. This part of the study successfully found a framework for testing the level of comfort with foreign cultures in multicultural workplaces and suitably tested for goodness of fit and reliability, both of exploratory factor analysis (EFA) and confirmatory factor analysis (CFA).

One reason for lesser errors noticed at the stage of CFA points to correct identification of observed variables by focus groups at the very first place. This could be done with suitable use of literature findings as described in the initial chapters of the book. Therefore the observed variables or questionnaire questions were thoughtfully identified. Three countries cross cultural comparison could therefore be carried out on a larger sample with much more reliability. A sample size of 995 for the CFC model testing and 835 for three countries cross cultural analysis was quite sufficient.

In this part of the study main objective was to analyze the results of the methodology used in the previous part of this chapter, and draw inferences from the data with respect to studying the significant or nonsignificant effects of the country and other control variables identified. Also a framework was devised to score the three countries on CFC. For this study several statistical techniques were used to analyze the quantitative data. The correlation between control variables and among CFC scales had been analyzed separately. The effect of 'country' on CFC scales had been tested along with the presence of other control variables like – education level, age group, income group and others.

Inter-correlation between control variables

This section of the study analyzed the sample and respondent data for correlation between 'control variables' and also tests the validity of the questionnaire used for sample data. As could be seen from the results of this exercise, it was found that some correlation between 'gender' and 'income group' and holds true for all countries except *Italy*. It may also be noted that the correlation between 'income group' and 'age group' was rather high in case of *India* than other countries. However, there was no significant correlation between 'age group' and any other control variable, except 'income group'. In 'income group' also, some correlation was there in case of *India* and *Portugal* but not in the case of *Italy*. There was no significant correlation between 'education level' and other control variables except the control variable 'country'. It may also be noticed that there was any significant correlation between variable 'country' and other control variables like 'income group', 'age group' and 'education level'. However, in totality the correlation between several control variable was not very large.

Overall, it was found 'CFC scales' are more inter correlated in the case of *Portugal* and *Italy* than in the case of *India*. Therefore, it may be noted that while there is no significant correlation among control variables there does exist some correlation among CFC scales. However, such correlation is obvious and is not really very high.

Impact of different control variables in CFC model

In the previous sections, we analyzed the reliability and validity of the CFC scales and the subscales of the intercultural comfort of employees at the multicultural workplaces in *India*, *Italy* and *Portugal*, samples were now compared and tested for equality, using 2 Ways ANOVA. These comparisons and testing were also done in the presence of control variables such as 'gender', 'income group', 'age group' and 'education level' among the three samples. Scale wise impact of different control variables is summarized and inferences were derived.

In this part of the study we had consolidated all the information we had gathered from the comprehensive survey based study and tried to find mean differences among three countries on different dimensions of intercultural comfort dynamics among team members of international project teams at multinational firms. Here a conceptual question arised. That is why we expect the behavior of employees of multinational firms to be different from country to country in terms of their comfort level with foreign cultures. Firstly the cultures of these countries are surely different as it emerges from several cross cultural studies of the past, notably that of *Hofstede* (1980)[5]. These cultural differences are likely to have a major impact on such behaviors. Secondly, the baseline characteristics, including demographic factors could also differ. The educational system for examples could be different in terms of encouragement of creativity, fostering of a questioning attitude and so on[6]. A collective through - line in a country could also be the result of a certain underlying cultural pattern within that country, and many such patterns could emerge across countries[6].

It must further be noted that apart from country, other control variables as identified in the earlier sections of the study, such as gender, 'income group' etc. could also affect these underlying patterns within the country so that overall country differences in terms of comfort with foreign cultures (CFC) among countries are expected. Such differences in underlying patterns could also emerge within the countries and differences in terms of CFC within nations among different geographical areas cannot be ruled out. However, an attempt had been made to study intra country differences in terms of intercultural comfort among large cities in a particular nation (as described later in this chapter). As it appears for the purpose of the current study, such differences within countries can be assumed to be negligible.

Scale wise results are presented in tabular form for easy visualization. We have used a 'two way' approach to study these differences. First, we have listed country wise significance of observed mean differences using ANOVA and post hoc tests (*Tukey's*) (table 8.4). Secondly, we have calculated 'estimated marginal means' of CFC scale as dependable variables for control variable 'country' in the presence of all other control variables as described and identified in the previous part of this chapter.

The observed mean differences in terms of country effects

Before we study the CFC scale wise mean differences, let us summarize observed mean differences (from *Tukey's* post hoc test) as given in table 8.4

Table 8.4: Observed mean differences (based on post hoc test *Tukey's*)

Scale	India – Italy	India – Portugal	Italy – Portugal
S1	Not Significant	Significant	Significant
S2	Significant	Significant	Significant
S3	Significant	Significant	Not Significant
S4	Significant	Significant	Not Significant
S5	Significant	Significant	Not Significant
S6	Significant	Significant	Significant
S7	Significant	Not Significant	Significant

S8	Significant	Not Significant	Significant
S10	Not Significant	Significant	Significant
S11	Not Significant	Significant	Significant
ST1	Not Significant	Not Significant	Not Significant
ST2	Significant	Not Significant	Significant
ST3	Significant	Significant	Not Significant
ST4	Not Significant	Not Significant	Significant
ST5	Significant	Significant	Not Significant

As can be seen from table 8.4, it can be inferred that observed mean differences more or less vary significantly from country to country (at least in terms of 3 countries included in the study)

The data analysis described in this part of the chapter for three inter country study, could successfully estimate the impact of different control variables on the latent variables identified in the CFC model. These latent variables were obtained from the observed variables used as survey instrument questions. These latent variables formed the structure of the CFC model which was analyzed in this research to study the impact of identified control variables the prime of which is 'country' as a control variable. As it is clear from the analysis of this part, 'country' has significant impact on the latent variables (CFC scales). Therefore the level of comfort with foreign cultures in multinational firms, clearly vary from country to country.

Study of the intra country effect

In this part of the book, a study has been described which attempted to propose a framework to test the level of comfort, of the local cultures with culturally different persons in an intra country setting and suggest certain parameters which plays an important role in deciding 'level of comfort', so that project managers may be trained to better manage their cross cultural teams and ensure their success in a multicultural environment in the national context. More specifically, this part of study tried to identify variables which may have a direct relationship with this level of comfort including city effect, level of education, age group, gender and income group. In this part of the study only a limited number of large cities in three countries have been taken up, where authors could find resources to collect survey based data from a scientifically designed sample for the inquiry. A framework for questionnaire design is based on theoretical foundations as described in the earlier sections and is tested. While the choice of cities included in the study was a result of respondent's demographic profiles who opted to take online surveys and the subsequent consolidation of data to see which cities give sufficient number of responses and where the data analysis is feasible for this study. Fortunately the results of such consolidation were very suitable to this research since limited number of cities in these three countries which could be included in this research were representative of culturally diverse and distant parts.

Definitions:

Intra country level of comfort - In this chapter, intra country level of comfort refers to the ease of working between team members belonging to regional cultures and those from culturally different groups, in multicultural teams working with large national and international firms.

Culturally different persons – Culturally different persons herein refers to those team members in multicultural teams who belong to cultural groups coming from distant places as well as those from foreign cultures (all in a national context though).

Research design and modeling

This part of the study used comfort with a culturally different questionnaire (CCD questionnaire was derived along with the CFC questionnaire developed in earlier sections almost parallel. It very much resembles with the CFC questionnaire questions except in the context) to study respondents from eight major cities in each of the three countries – *India, Italy* and *Portugal*. The response data were mostly collected using the online questionnaire. The respondents were mostly in the 23 to 48 age group category having been part of cross cultural teams in international and national projects and working with multinational and large national companies on projects involving cross cultural teams in their respective countries. EFA was carried out on the CCD questionnaire to identify latent variables (CCD scales). Control variables like – city, gender, income group, education level, age group were identified. ANOVA was applied to verify the impact of control variables on CCD scales.

Sources and types of data

Data was collected using online survey instruments developed in a national context for three countries involving respondents working for large organizations in culturally diverse project teams. Primary data were collected with the help of research collaborators in three countries, namely – *India, Portugal* and *Italy*. The data were in response to a survey instrument used for the research. The data were collected using *a Likert scale* of 1 to 5 similar to the one used in earlier sections of the research. Data was collected using online questionnaires administered with the help of research collaborators in two countries and by the authors.

Sample description

The sample surveyed with the aid of CCD questionnaire developed for the study (on the same line as the CFC questionnaire), consisted of respondents from eight large cities in each of the three countries. Each of the respondents working with large organizations had either worked or were working in a cross-cultural project team. The respondents were selected based on their profiles from different sources and through invitations by authors and research collaborators to take the online survey. Since a number of collaborators helped with the collection of data from different cities it was not possible to control respondents of which cities will take part in the survey and in what numbers. Table 8.5 gives a description of the overall sample detail city wise.

Table 8.5: Participating Respondents by City of Residence and Country

India								
City	Bangal ore	Chandi garh	Chenn ai	Delhi	Jaipur	Kolkat a	Luckn ow	Mumb ai	Total
Nos	85 (17%)	35 (7%)	35 (7%)	102 (21%)	45 (9%)	45 (9%)	72 (15%)	75 (15%)	494 (100%)
Portugal								
City	Aveiro	Braga	Castel o Branco	Evora	Leiria	Lisbon	Maia	Porto	Total
Nos	45 (11%)	49 (12%)	35 (8%)	40 (10%)	40 (10%)	75 (18%)	50 (12%)	85 (20%)	419 (100%)
Italy								
City	Floren ce	Genov a	Milan	Palerm o	Rome	Torino	Trevis o	Trieste	Total
Nos	42 (12%)	34 (10%)	32 (9%)	30 (9%)	26 (7%)	33 (9%)	76 (22%)	79 (22%)	352 (100%)

At the last stage of data collection those cities were included in the research where the numbers of respondents were sufficient enough to enable the data analysis. Thus, a systematic approach coupled with a convenient approach to sampling have been used

As it appears from the results, 'gender' is an important control variable since it may indirectly affect the level of comfort between different cultures at multicultural workplaces. It may be noted that questionnaire administered covered fairly good gender ratio among respondents in each city. Although there is a tilt towards male respondents, but the same was inevitable in an international study of this type. 'Income group' may also have an impact on the level of comfort among different cultural groups and is another important control variable. There are two distinct groups among respondents one of the 'higher income level' and another of 'average income or below an income level'. 'Average income' group accounts for the largest group among the sample. Therefore study had merged the 'average income' and 'below average income' group in order to rationalize the respondent's income group ratio. It may be noted that there was some correlation between the 'income group' and 'gender' variables as also between 'income group' and 'age group'. It was true for each city except *Italy*. There may also be an impact on 'age group' on intercultural level of comfort of respondents. The sample seemed to have fairly good composition of age group, although in case of *India*, the sample comprised of a comparatively younger age group. In case of *Portugal* and *Italy*, a significantly higher percentage of respondents belongs to 31 to 40 years category. However, these differences were inevitable and were the result of differences in demographic composition of the countries studied. Overall, there seemed to be no reason to believe that the age group composition as given in the sample for the current study was likely to affect the accuracy of intercultural comfort level results.

The sample contained a significantly higher percentage of respondents belonging to 'educational level' having a master's level education. However the sample still contained significant number of respondents from other educational groups.

Method used

The study used a four part methodology as used in the previous chapters. The methodology consisted of

1. Survey instrument development

2. Exploratory factor analysis on dataset 1 with IBM SPSS Statistics Base

3. Confirmatory factor analysis (CFA) and structural equation modeling (SEM) on dataset 2 (i.e., confirming correlations and

inferred causal relationships among factors) to obtain a model for 'comfort with culturally different' (CCD model)

4. Cross cultural comparison of data using CCD questionnaire obtained from above '3 stage' methodology.

Questionnaire Design

The questionnaire administered to the sample respondents in each country, consisted of two parts containing observed variables, similar to CFC questionnaire used in earlier sections. These observed variables have been derived conceptually as well as from *Delphi* technique using a two stage iteration method, and tested for validity and reliability by the authors using both EFA and CFA using structural equation modeling similar to the one used in the earlier section. First part of the questionnaire contains general CCD questions which can be answered by each respondent. The second part contains conditional questions. A third section of the questionnaire contains socio demographic questions, to acquire background information from the participating persons and related to factors like gender, age, nationality, educational level, income group, city of residence etc.

The three countries intra – country cross cultural comparison based on city effects was successfully done using a methodology perfected and described in the earlier chapters of this book. The comfort with culturally different persons among team members of multicultural teams in the national context traversed the same path as in previous chapters, as far as methodology is concerned. The analysis of baseline characteristics gave a balanced view of the sample design.

One of the major assumptions of this study had been the assumed insignificance of intra cultural differences. As it came out to the most important criticism of *Hofstede's* model was the assumption of the homogeneous society at national level [7]. Critics have concluded that *Hofstede* was interested in making a model which is universally accepted and that his model is at best a functional model [7]. In the present study these criticisms had been used to conclude that a supporting study of intra country cultural differences (with reference to CFC or in this case Comfort with Culturally different (CCD)) in geographically and culturally diverse countries like *India*, *Italy* and *Portugal*, would reduce any criticism with respect to the methodology used for comparing nations on CFC. As described in last chapter therefore a methodology had been used to suggest suitable CCD survey instrument on the lines of the CFC survey instrument, and data are collected from the large cities of these three countries. This data had been already validated and had been tested for suitability for the given survey instrument. In this part of the chapter we will describe the analysis of this data to see if there exists any influence of geographical locations of sub-cultures on the 'level of comfort' and impact of other identified control variables like gender, income group, education level and age group.

CCD model and CCD scales

The CCD scales (latent variables) were identified using EFA and CFA of all responses. Individual countries' responses were also tested using the EFA. In CFA, structural equation modeling gave the same results in case of data from individual countries. Due to a large number of results from each country in CFA, the SEM results were not included in this section. Moreover the SEM results were very similar to results obtained in the previous chapter.

In an earlier section of this chapter, we had argued about the reliability and validity of the scales and subscales of the intercultural comfort of employees at the multicultural workplaces in *India, Italy* and *Portugal* in the national and regional context, samples were now compared and tested for equality in this section, using *Univariate Analysis of Variance*. These comparisons and testing were also done in the presence of control variables such as gender, income group, age group and education level among the eight samples in each of the 3 countries. One of the problems associated with using surveys based on *a Likert scale* for cross cultural analysis related to the differences of answering pattern in different countries by the respondents. However, looking at the reliability and validity analysis on the data and eight samples, it can be safely assumed that no such answering effect was likely to be there in the results.

Impact of City and other Control Variables

The results for the scores of each of the eight cities in *India* and those of the differences between the eight, in terms of the city and control variables indicated that the situation for CCD scale ST5 in the case of *Italy* and *Portugal* is also almost same. There is no significant city effect and any other control variable effect in both cases on CCD scale.

Conclusion

The primary data based inter country studies provided us with an impressive set of latent and observed variables which were further tested using CFA and the model was further refined. This fine tuned model provided a great insight into the phenomenon of 'level of

CFC' which will be discussed in later chapters.

The analysis of the data in the last part of this chapter indicated rather not very surprising results. It tends to indicate that in none of the three countries comprehensively studied in this chapter, there is any significant city effect on the latent variables (CCD scales) of the CCD model. That is a confirmation of the validity of a major assumption of Hofstede's model and that of many other social scientists who made similar intra country assumptions to carry our intercontinental cross cultural comparison in different sectors and settings of commercial and noncommercial organizations. However, it may be noted that the current work confined itself to the study of multinational firms or large commercial workplaces and therefore may not reflect on the similar or dissimilar pattern of societal behavior outside the MNE or large commercial workplaces. Further, it is also concluded that the impact of other control variables like gender, income group, age group and 'educational levels' is also not highly significant in intra country context but need to be studied in detail in cases of inter country comparisons.

Suggested questions for discussion:

1) Based on the results of the EFA and CFA, what are the latent variables which strongly explain the 'level of CFC' at multicultural workplaces? Discuss these variables with examples.

2) What are the important control variables other than 'country' which may influence the 'level of CFC' at multinational workplaces? Discuss these control variables and their significance vis-a-vis the prime control variable 'country' as described in this chapter.

3) What is the explanation for non significant effect of 'city' as a control variable in describing the CFC phenomenon? In other words, why the intra country effect is negligible on CFC? Discuss.

4) What kinds of different learning can be drawn from the results of the primary data study on 'level of CFC'? Discuss.

Notes:

1. Olsson, U. (1979). Maximum likelihood estimation of the polyphonic correlation coefficient. *Psychometrika*, 44, 443-460.

2. McDonald, R.P. (1999). *Test theory: A unified treatment. Mahwah*, NJ: Lawrence Erlbaum.

3. Ten Berge, JMF, Snijders, TAB & Zegers, FE (1981). Computational aspects of the greatest lower bound to reliability and constrained minimum trace factor analysis. *Psychometrika*, 46, 201-213.

4. Geertz, C. (1983). *Local knowledge*. NY: Basic Books.

5. Hofstede, G. (1980). *Culture's consequences: International differences in work-related values*. Beverly Hills, CA: Sage.

6. Manakutty, S. (2010). Effects of Nationality on the approaches to learning and studying, p44, in *Cross –cultural approaches to learning and studying*, McMillan, *India*

7. McSweeney, Brendan (2002). Hofstede's Model of National Cultural Differences and Their Consequences: A Triumph of Faith - A Failure of Analysis. *Human Relations* 55 (1)

Online resources for this chapter, available at:
http://www.vijeshjain.com/books/multinational-workplaces/resources/chapter-8

9. MULTINATIONAL WORKPLACES: WAR OF CULTURALLY SEASONED MINDS

In this chapter, different outcomes of the previous chapters have been collated to draw inferences from those results. The significances of these results have been arranged in a manner to draw a useful understanding of the accounts of the studies conducted in writing this book. This chapter is more of a summary of interpretation of whatever has been discussed in this book and inferences are obtained to postulate certain conclusions, recommendations and suggestions.

Cross cultural studies described in this book on the inquiry of 'level of CFC' have explored several dimensions of intercultural comfort at multinational workplaces. The important focus of these studies has been on the people's issues in multicultural work teams rather than on looking at the 'prescriptions and control' dynamics for team success. These studies have successfully established that level of comfort, of local cultures with foreign cultures varies from country to country. On the same note assumption that 'such variation of comfort level is an international phenomenon and intra country cultural differences in terms of comfort with culturally different people are non-existent', is also proved. We have also looked at the implications of the studies in terms of what multinational firms can do to ensure the work team's success. Referring to the several inferences drawn based on both published and surveys generated data, these studies collectively confirmed the complexity of the cross cultural comfort process in international project teams at multinational firms. These therefore provided most valuable information on the phenomenon of cross cultural comfort, especially the level of comfort, of local cultures with foreign cultures (CFC).

What these studies highlight is the need for considerably more research focusing on the people's issues in multicultural teams at the workplaces of multinational firms. With the growth in globalization, project managers in international project teams will need to be more culturally sensitive and competent to handle more and more culturally diverse teams and culturally seasoned members. Thereby we can be better assured of the benefits of multiculturalism in international work teams which will result in better ideas, new approaches to problem solving and excellence in the international projects. It is clear that multiculturalism at multinational workplaces will bring forth need for better understanding and expectations regarding team management. This chapter also discusses the conclusions of the different studies as described in the earlier chapters.

The conclusions of the CFC studies as described in this book

Conclusion of a social science study like this is very difficult to obtain most scientifically. However, as *Michael Argyle* (1957)[1] writes "modern psychologists are more concerned with behavior, rather than the state of consciousness", therefore survey instruments like questionnaires, interviews and their statistical analysis can still interpret useful conclusions if done comprehensively. In this book, authors had tried to look at the inquiry from several angles and have objectively tested all assumptions, limitations and validated to the extent possible. In the following paragraphs, the authors have described some of the important conclusions which are the results of years of study on the topic as well as a series of brainstorming sessions with cross cultural experts, mentors, cross cultural students and foreign collaborators.

As can be seen from the preliminary CFC scores estimated using the published data there are countries in the world with 'high CFC scores' like *USA*, *India*, and *Tanzania* at one hand. At the same time, there are also countries with 'lower CFC scores' like *Japan* and *Denmark*. There are others with 'moderate CFC scores' like *South Korea* and *South Africa*. Therefore, there is a clear difference in level of CFC among several countries of the world. It is important to see the relationship between CFC scores estimated in the above study and those predicted by *Hofstede's* existing cultural dimensions. This comparative analysis is given in following paragraphs.

Comparison of preliminary CFC scores with Hofstede's model

It is important to note that 'low CFC score of *Japan*' seems to align with the predictions of *Hofstede's* scores especially on UAI (Uncertainty Avoidance Index). A 'high score on UAI' of *Hofstede* indicates that *Japanese* culture is not easy or comfortable with the foreign cultures or foreigners in order to avoid any awkward outcome of such 'strange' interactions. However a 'high score on LTO' for *Japan* does not go well with low CFC scores in *Japan*. A 'high LTO score' should mean that the *Japanese* people should take a long term and pragmatic view of their interactions with foreigners and foreign cultures; thereby meaning they should be anxious to know more about cultural diversity which should be very helpful for *Japanese* culture in understanding different points of views expressed by different cultures of the world. At the same time low UAI countries like *Denmark* must show a more comfortable level with foreigners and foreign cultures. However, 'low CFC score' of *Denmark*, indicates the situation otherwise.

Similarly a high PDI and Low UAI country like *China* must show large comfort with foreigners and foreign culture. The 'CFC score' for *China*, *however* indicate different situation. An average score of *China* on CFC does not go well with the high score of LTO. 'High CFC scores' of *the US* and *Canada*, does not match with a 'low LTO score' but go well with a moderate score on UAI. *South Korea's* 'high UAI score' should predict a 'lower CFC scores'. This is not the case. *Hungary's* 'High CFC Score' does not align with the 'high UAI score'. Therefore, in most of the cases, *Hofstede's* existing dimensions does not predict the score on CFC. A comparative chart of all the *Hofstede's* dimensions along with the estimated CFC scores is given in table 9.1 below.

Table 9.1: Comparison of CFC scores with *Hofstede's* Scores

	CFC[a]	PDI[b]	IDV[c]	MAS[d]	UAI[c]	LTO[d]
Australia	55	36	90	61	51	31
Brazil	57	69	38	49	76	65
Canada	70	39	80	52	48	23
China	55	80	20	66	30	118
Denmark	33	18	74	16	23	46
France	63	68	71	43	86	39
Germany	59	35	67	66	65	31
Hungary	70	46	80	88	82	50
India	76	77	48	56	40	61
Iran	71	58	41	43	59	
Italy	48	50	76	70	75	34

Japan	**40**	54	46	95	92	80
Kenya	**57**					
New Zealand	**62**	22	79	58	49	30
Poland	**71**	68	60	64	93	32
Portugal	**55**	63	27	31	104	30
S. Korea	**53**	68	71	43	86	39
South Africa	**52**	49	65	63	49	
Sweden	**73**	31	71	5	29	20
Tanzania	**76**	70	25	40	50	30
UK	**66**	35	89	66	35	25
USA	**78**	40	91	62	46	29

[a] CFC   Comfort with Foreign Cultures
[b] PDI   Power Distance
[c] IDV   Individualism
[d] MAS   Masculinity
[e] UAI   Uncertainty Avoidance
[f] LTO   Long Term Orientation

A look at the above table clearly indicates that CFC scores based on research using the published data as input, does not align with the potential prediction of level of CFC by *Hofstede's* cultural dimension scores. A further study into correlation between *Hofstede's* scores on different dimensions and CFC scores as calculated, indicated that there does not exist any significant correlation between *Hofstede's* scores and CFC scores. These results and findings, therefore, are indicative of the diversity of the cultures of the world with respect to their propensity to accept the foreigners in their own countries. The cultural aspect of this type otherwise, may be difficult to assess by common knowledge and existing cultural studies. Therefore the results of the above kind will be helpful in making informed decisions, with respect to international strategic decisions for commercial or non commercial players and to manage international project teams in multinational firms.

Country ranks comparisons among different methods

Among the countries studied, it seems there are countries which are more comfortable for foreigners and foreign cultures than others. It may be noted that among the countries studied, *India* ranks most unfavorably. There could be cultural and historical reasons which make local culture in

India comparatively less comfortable with foreign cultures. A detailed study on specific country differences later threw more light on these differences. It appeared that *Scandinavian* countries like *Sweden* are quite different culturally from most of the other nations of the world.

It may be noted that the pilot survey based study was done on a smaller pilot sample and is indicative only. However the study gave an insight into the world trend in the comfort level of local cultures with foreign cultures. It also listed scale wise differences among the countries studied. Most of the latent variables associated with level of CFC were derived using suitable statistical methods. The ranking of countries according to their CFC scores based on a CFC model designed for use with published data was compared with ranking obtained from another CFC model designed for survey based pilot data. A total of 22 countries was studied in simple conceptual CFC modeling, while nine countries were studied in the primary data based pilot study. Table 9.2 below gives the comparison of nine common countries of these two studies.

Table 9.2: Comparison of ranks of countries from primary and secondary data (pilot study)

Comfort Ranks from Published Data			Rank from Survey Data (from pilot study)		
Rank			Rank 1*	Rank 2**	Name of the country
1	USA		1	2.5	USA
2	India		2	1	Sweden
3	Sweden		3	4	UK
4	UK		4	5	Portugal
5	Brazil		5	6	Brazil
6	Kenya		6	2.5	China
7	China		7	7	Kenya
8	Portugal		8	8	Italy
9	Italy		9	9	India

*Rank obtained from rank scores
**Rank obtained from mean values

It may be noted from table 9.2 that ranks of the countries from both the CFC studies reasonably matched with the exception of *India* and *Portugal*. The reason for *India* emerging as better ranked using published data may be due to the inherent bias of the *Delphi* teams most of the members being of *Indian* origin. Reasons for the differences in rank of *Portugal* need further investigation. It may be noted that the ranks of the countries in the above comparison were based on either published data or a pilot smaller study. A detailed study was done in three countries – *India, Portugal* and *Italy* offers a better understanding of the overall ranks.

Conclusions from three country comprehensive study

A three country comprehensive study took into account survey data of a sample of more than 800 responses. Explained variance was studied on important control variables to see the significance of differences of 'level of CFC'. The share of explained variance was rather high for most of the results. More than 30% of variance on the CFC scales S2, S3, S4 and ST5 was explained by 'country' variable. Similarly, more than 20% of the variance on CFC scales S1, S5, S8, S11, ST1 and ST3 was explained by 'country' variable. On other CFC scales too, the effect of 'country' variable was rather high, except on ST2. This is conceptually explainable (Stereotypes of 'low and average income group' about 'high income group' are likely to be rather uniform across countries). More than 10% of variance on CFC scales S1, S2, S3, S4, and S5 was explained by 'gender' effect. More than 15% of variance on CFC scales S7 and S8 was explained by 'income group' variable. More than 10% of variance on CFC scales S1, S5, S6, ST1, and ST3 was explained by 'age group' control variable. More than 10% of variance on CFC scales S5, S6, S7, S8, S11, ST1 and ST2 were explained by 'education level'. Overall 'country' as a control variable played most important role in explaining variance on most CFC scales. 'Country' effect on CFC scale S7 was rather low. This can be partly explained by the fact that religious sentiments go beyond political borders and reflect a seemingly global egalitarian society of cultural groups less affected by differences of 'nationality'. In comparison, the effect of other control variables on overall CFC scales was rather low.

A rather high shares of explained variance of scales S3 and S4 due to 'gender' variable may require further investigation into the phenomenon. Similarly a higher share of explained variance on CFC scales S7 and S8 due to 'income group' may also require further investigation. Higher explanation of 'education level' variable on the variance of CFC scales S8 and S11 can be attributed to higher levels of global awareness among more educated respondents. However the same 'higher explanation' of variance of CFC scale S7, due to 'education level' variable may require further investigation.

Finally, post hoc tests (*Tukey's* Test) (see table 8.4 in chapter 8) indicated 'observed mean differences' among '*India* & *Italy*' was not significant while '*India* & *Portugal*' and '*Italy* & *Portugal*' differences were significant for dependent variables S1, S10 and S11 in the presence of each of other control variables. For dependent variables S2 and S6, 'observed mean differences' were significant in case of 'all pairs' of countries in the presence of each of other control variables. Similarly, in case of S3, S4, S5, ST3 and ST5 'mean differences' between *'Italy* & *Portugal'* were not significant. In case of S7, S8 and ST2, 'observed mean differences' between *'India* & *Portugal'* were not significant. 'Observed mean differences' are insignificant for any of the pair of countries in case of ST1. In case of ST4, only *'Italy* & *Portugal'* 'observed mean differences' were significant. This indicated there are overall significant 'observed mean differences' among all countries studied on all scales except for scale - ST1.

Some of the interesting inferences which emerged from these results were that higher income group stereotypes towards lower or average income group, although vary from country to country, did not differ significantly. Similarly willingness to socialize with foreigners and views about globalization varied from country to country and the observed mean difference was also high among all three countries studied on country to country basis. Similarly, gender stereotype among women about men was not very significantly different from country to country except in the case of *Italy* and *Portugal* while there was a strong country effect on this scale too. In all other cases country effect was rather high and observed mean differences are significant in most cases. The immediate conclusion of these results was that most of the CFC scales would vary from country to country and therefore these scales provided a strong base to measure level of CFC among countries.

Ranking of three countries based on the overall CFC scales

In order to do the analysis we had divided the set of CFC scales in two groups – general CFC scales and conditional CFC scales (stereotype scales). Therefore first group represented CFC scales S1 to S11 (CFC Scales Group 1) and second group referred to CFC scales ST1 to ST5 (CFC Scales Group 2). The reason for dividing these two groups was obvious. As we had seen in our methodology we had divided the observed variables associated with these groups separately so that the different treatment was necessary for the variables associated with these two groups. As it appeared from details of significance of mean differences discussed above and in chapter 8, and also seeing the level of CFC scales for three countries in group 1 latent variables, *Portugal* seemed to be most comfortable to foreigners, followed by *Italy* and *India*. Doing the same analysis for Group 2 CFC variables, we found that *India* had the least stereotypes, followed by *Portugal* and *Italy*.

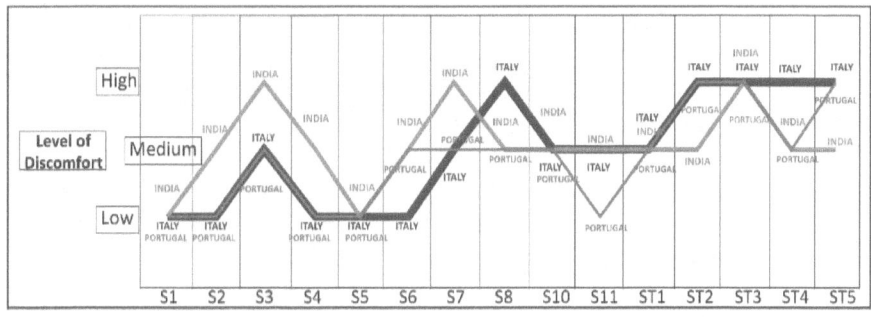

Figure 9.1: Chart showing level of CFC scale scores for each country

Therefore the ranking of countries for two groups of CFC scales was founded as given in table 9.3.

Table 9.3: Ranks of countries from three country primary data

CFC Scales	Group 1 CFC variables	Group 2 CFC variables
Rank1	Portugal	India
Rank2	Italy	Portugal
Rank3	India	Italy

CFC Scores for three countries

Based on these CFC scales of the final CFC model we had calculated the CFC scores on a scale of 0 to 100 using the survey data. These scores are given in table 9.4

Table 9.4: CFC scores based on 3 country comprehensive studies

CFC Scores	India	Italy	Portugal
General Scores	56	67	71
Stereotype Scores	55	40	44
Composite Scores	56	64	68

The composite scores were calculated by giving 1/8th weight to stereotype scores based on a first set of general variables and 3 stereotype variables combined as another set. A higher score indicates a higher level of CFC. Now looking at the fact that group 1 CFC variables (general variables) represented a larger set of latent variables, and giving higher importance to the workplace behavior represented by group 1 variables, the overall ranking of the level of comfort on CFC emerged as – *Portugal*, *Italy* and *India*. Thus, among the three countries studied *Portugal* emerged as most comfortable to foreign cultures and *India* as the least.

These results go well with the findings of survey based pilot study. Therefore the idea that there exist certain observed and latent cultural variables which can describe the variation of level of comfort of local cultures with foreign cultures in cross cultural project teams working with multinational firms holds true. At the same time the level of comfort, of local cultures with foreign cultures, cross cultural project teams working with multinational companies, varies from country to country also holds true. Conclusions of the three nation's intra country study of intercultural differences. The three nation's intra country study conclusively proved the assumption that intra country cultural differences in terms of level of CFC among employees of large organization working in multicultural teams do not vary significantly from city to city (i.e. City of residence as control variable). Therefore, idea that the level of comfort, of local cultures with culturally different persons in cross cultural project teams working with national and multinational firms does not vary from one city to another city within a particular geographically and culturally large nation, holds true.

Managerial Implications of the study

The proposition of the CFC as a new cultural dimension provides new insights into useful cultural aspects of different countries. The above dimension will add new meaning to the overall picture of the cultural profiles of the countries for several purposes, including those for managerial decision making at multinational firms particularly with respect to multicultural work teams. This cultural dimension explains a special aspect of the culture which is directly related to the survival of foreign businesses and businessmen in an alien country. The above results can variously be used in several kinds of managerial applications and subject areas like

1. International human resources management,
2. Post merger integration,
3. Business entry decisions,
4. Parent – subsidiary relationship management etc.

The CFC scales suggested in this research can be used to measure CFC scores of different countries in order for project managers to better understand the group comfort dynamics of cross cultural teams they are managing. However a survey based data is required for each country to be scored. Further the study serves as a strong base for multinational firms to understand and provide cultural sensitivities and cross cultural management capabilities to team managers. The study also provides an exposure to multinational firms' approach to adopt practices which maintain a balance of

1) Global competitiveness,
2) Multinational flexibility and
3) Building the global learning capabilities

One of the related implications for project managers working in multicultural teams is that they need to spend extra hours to find ways to manage intercultural discomfort among cultural groups in their project teams. It means they should be spending more time talking than being on the desk. They often need to talk with the team members about the issues and problems arising out of intercultural discomfort and find collective ways to find solutions directly or indirectly related to the level of comfort of the native cultures with foreign cultures.

Success of multicultural team does not lie in just the delivery of the project in time. It goes beyond just that to exceed client's expectations and making an impression. To achieve just that an understanding of the type described in this study related to level of CFC, can go a long way in maximizing the client experience through results coming from effective teams with least communications issues, least conflicts, great cohesiveness, alignment, higher integration, smoother information flow, better understanding of project goals and targets. One of the important areas which will benefit most through an understanding of CFC is the building of high level of trust among cross cultural groups in multicultural teams in multinational firms.

Limitations of the studies

The studies discussed in this book are however limited to the educated respondents, who are reasonably well to do and working at decent jobs in multinational firms across the countries. Therefore the results of the studies may not reflect the comfort dynamics of the entire sections of local cultures with foreign cultures on a societal or national level. A very large study can only be conclusive on that scale. Further the cultural behavior of the type discussed in this study is fairly dynamic in nature and therefore cultural sensitivities are likely to vary among countries at least at the business level over prolonged periods. Therefore the results of the kind as emerged from these studies are likely to vary over time. It is therefore may be important to carry out further studies of the above types after say every 5 to 8 years in order to update CFC scores.

Recommendations from the studies

The following recommendations have been collated based on different categories of the targeted users and audience of these studies. The authors have identified the potential users of this study as-

1. Social science researchers and research scholars of similar topics,
2. Industry users,
3. Academics having teaching interests in the subject of the study and finally
4. The students of cross cultural management.

For industrial users

Senior project managers or heads of international project teams will do well to understand thoroughly the nuisances of managing multicultural teams, especially with respect to intercultural comfort dynamics as discussed in this study. Some of the important recommendations for these managers working with multinational firms are-

1) Team leaders need to spend substantially more time in discussing issues and problems more than doing desk work.
2) This should ensure avoiding misunderstandings related to cross cultural differences among team members.
3) It is clear that face to face dialogue rather than written instructions ensures ease of work and avoidance of misgivings and misunderstandings.
4) Team leaders will do better to focus their attention more on the trans-national cultural differences rather than national sub cultural differences as it appears from the current study that national subcultures carry with them a certain amount of national commonality.
5) Team leaders need to focus on right and clear understanding of project information down to the last members of the team irrespective of their cultural background. Sometimes due to cultural differences, some of the team members or groups are left with less or no information on the vital aspects of the work in hand.

6) Team leaders need to build confidence among team members and create an environment of trust and affinity irrespective of their cultural preferences and background.

7) Team leaders should ensure transparency in their decisions and unbiased attitude towards team members with respect to allocation of roles and responsibilities. For example, certain categories of team members should not expect a biased and 'by default' behavior by team leaders.

8) Team leaders must encourage all team members to respect each other and their ways of living irrespective of their cultural background.

9) Team leaders need to encourage higher levels of collectivism rather than individualism in order to mitigate the adverse effects of varying levels of comfort among culturally different persons in the team.

10) Another recommendation based on these studies relates to the conflict management. Conflict as such is related to intercultural discomfort. In order to understand conflict, it is important to understand that there are two categories of conflict – positive and negative. Both can emerge from intercultural discomfort. Carrying out day to day work, while managing positive conflict, team leaders can channelize the team members to work in a certain way which maximizes the team result. But negative conflicts need to be resolved in the shortest possible time. For this most important thing is to find out why a particular conflict has occurred.

11) And lastly team leaders must highlight to the team members why he or she has decided to resolve the issues in certain ways and why it is important for the best results for the project in hand.

For research scientists and research scholars

These studies also open up a plethora of opportunities for research in the domain of 'intercultural comfort at workplaces'. A good starting point will be to study the effect of 'country to country pairs' on different comfort scales with the overall level of CFC among team members. It means that it may be investigated if the level of CFC varies among different combinations of pairs of countries, in the intercultural interactions. It may be further investigated if the 'cultural distance' among different pairs of countries may have an impact on the level of CFC among employees of a unique pair of country interaction. Another area of interest for the researchers would be to work on the 'ease of work' model similar to 'comfort model' suggested in the current study. The new model related to 'ease of work' dynamics may also focus on issues beyond cross cultural comfort and may include issues like dominant personality traits in different cultures, work ethics, work goals etc.

Academics and trainers

These studies also provide new opportunities for trainers and teachers, especially those working in cross cultural domains. The specific trainings related to understanding the intercultural group comfort dynamics can be designed based on the comfort model suggested in these studies. Moreover, skills related to handling 'culturally charged workplaces conflicts' can be imparted to management students interested in taking up international business careers. These studies can also be part of syllabus of cross cultural management courses. While handling multicultural groups in workplaces of multinational firms, the studies can also serve as 'do's and don't for the 'team leader trainings'. Certain certification courses can also be devised using these studies to certify team leaders being capable of handling transnational work teams.

Suggested questions for discussion:

1) What are the tools and techniques which multinational firms and team leaders can use to address people's issues of the workplace management? Discuss.
2) What are the important areas of multicultural team management, which need to be frequently addressed to fully exploit the benefits of multiculturalism in work teams? Discuss.
3) Why do managers of today need to spend more time in talking to subordinates than engaging themselves in deskwork? Discuss.
4) What is the importance of clear and accurate communication in multicultural team management? Discuss.
5) What kinds of leadership traits are desirable for effective multicultural team management in the light of the conclusions of CFC studies? Discuss.

Notes:

1. Argyle, M., (1957). The Scientific Study of Social Behavior, p13

Online resources for this chapter, available at:
http://www.vijeshjain.com/books/multinational-workplaces/resources/chapter-9

10. CFC AMONG COUNTRY PAIRS

Till now in this book our focus had been discussing about the variation of the 'level of CFC' among local and any overseas or alien cultures and also to locate other control variables which affect 'level of that kind of CFC'. In this chapter we have described another study carried out by authors mainly focusing on mapping the variation of 'level of CFC' among local cultures and the specific cultural groups originating from specific nations at multinational workplaces. For example, in a particular national culture, the propensity of CFC for the local cultures may vary according to the country of origin of the foreign teammates. To understand the concept, a new theoretical framework was identified and proposed to deal with this type of country to country 'level of CFC' or CFC among country pairs. The proposed model was tested on 14 local cultures (one part of the pair) with 14 destination cultures (the second part of the pair). The observed variations indicate that country to country level of CFC does vary from one local culture to another and there are interesting patterns in such kinds of mapping.

The objective of this research study was to map the level of CFC of a set of employees from MNEs in 'respondent' nations with other teammates coming from different cultural backgrounds from a set of 'destination' nations or regions of the world. For example, this study allowed us to compare the level of CFC of *Italians* with individuals coming from, say, *North America* or from *Western Europe* or *Middle East*. We can also compare, for instance, the varying level of cultural comfort of *Australians* with persons coming from *African* nations, *South Asia* or *Central Asia*. In the current study, we tested that such 'intercultural comfort' among different combinations of cultural pairs when compared should be different. Another aspect studied about such intercultural comfort among different cultural pairs related to test if there is a pattern in such paired intercultural comfort levels. This study tested above ideas on the data collected from multinational employees coming from 14 different 'respondent' national cultures with a set of such employee coming from 14 'destination' regions. The method used to test above ideas in the current study is elaborated in following paragraphs.

Methodology

There can be several conceivable variables which can define culture to the culture level of CFC. The approaches of defining these can be different. Current study took into consideration a perception scaling and consultative method to devise variables (scales) which could define a CFC model capable of explaining the level of CFC among country pairs, which was the primary theme of the this study. The cross cultural analysis of the research into such culture to culture comfort was done on a set of more than 15 countries / regions of the world using an online questionnaire, the data collection for which was supported by research collaborators in these countries/regions. The choice of these countries was the result of a collection of pilot data from an earlier international study already discussed in this book for determination of the locations for the data collection. The new questionnaire for this study was a result of a perception mapping and consultative exercise involving a 5 stage iteration based on *the Delphi technique* with the help of a group of 100 cross cultural experts and students on cross cultural management course. The resultant questionnaire is given in *Annexure* in table 10.1a.

The data were based on convenience sampling using approximately 650 responses from employees of multinational firms located in more than 15 countries. On review of the online data collected from these countries, it was found that many countries' numbers of respondents were insignificant to be considered. On final review it was observed that valid and sufficient responses were available from 14 respondent countries, namely -*Italy* (84), *Argentina* (31), *Australia* (32), *Canada* (32), *China* (40), *Germany* (38), *Japan* (32), *Nigeria* (32), *Pakistan* (35), *Saudi* Arabia (35), *U.K.* (45), *USA* (34), *India* (54) and *Portugal* (32). The questionnaire was further tested for repeatability, reliability and validity. The sample was spread to several companies and several verticals within organizations to avoid polarization of the same cultural group while responding to questions. The validity was established on almost 500 responses, which were selected on the basis of the origins of the responses and a reasonable count of responses from each country.

Lesser responses from a particular country or region were excluded from the sample data since it was not considered significant enough for the current study. A final sample of 556 responses made the basis for the study as described in Table 10.1.

Table 10.1: Sample structure of the cross cultural study

Name of the country	Sample Size	No of Males	No of Females
Italy	84	40 (48%)	44 (52%)
Argentina	31	10 (32%)	21 (68%)
Australia	32	12 (37%)	20 (63%)
Canada	32	11 (34%)	21 (66%)
China	40	25 (63%)	15 (37%)
Germany	38	13 (34%)	25 (66%)
Japan	32	15 (47%)	17 (53%)
Nigeria	32	20 (63%)	12 (27%)
Pakistan	35	28 (80%)	7 (20%)
Saudi Arabia	35	27 (77%)	8 (23%)
U.K.	45	20 (44%)	25 (56%)
USA	34	14 (41%)	20 (59%)
India	54	30 (55%)	24 (45%)
Portugal	32	15 (47%)	17 (53%)
Total	556	280 (50%)	276 (50%)

The respondents were asked to respond to the questions on a 5 point *Likert's* scale, higher score indicating 'lower level of CFC' of respondents with a specific 'alien culture' (hereinafter referred to as the 'destination culture'). All the responses to the new questionnaire were added to a single input sheet into SPSS program and 'mean scores' were compared to several questions with respect to corresponding destinations, with the independent variable as the 'respondent country'. The 'mean scores' were also compared for each question with respect to 14 'destinations'. For example, question related to the respondent's preference of employees of a particular cultural origin, as an employer, were compared and tabulated (see tables 10.2 to 10.15). All questions (a total of 7 questions) indicated the level of preference among respondents from a single respondent country and is given in rows in each table (table 10.2 to 10.15). The mean scores were tabulated in different tables for all 14 respondent countries. These questions acted as the different scales to understand the overall level of CFC with a particular 'destination' region. These scales were as per new questionnaire structure as discussed above.

Results and observations

Based on the above clustering of the items (CFC scales) in the new questionnaire, following insights were obtained with respect to comfort scales of questionnaire using the primary data from 556 respondents, across 14 countries.

Culture to Culture Comfort among Respondents from 14 Different Countries

Cultural preferences of respondents from 14 different countries vary on Culture to Culture Comfort scales across 14 regions of the world. Table 10.2 to 10.15 give a visual representation based on traits responses to 'cultural pairs scales' from respondents from these respondent countries.

Table 10.2: Mean comfort scores for respondents from Italy

ITALY	Q1	Q2	Q3	Q4	Q5	Q6	Q7	Mean
North America	2.07	2.02	1.88	2.04	1.89	1.99	1.76	1.95
Central America	2.48	2.27	2.21	2.36	2.30	2.40	1.79	2.26
South America	2.67	2.39	2.30	2.43	2.35	2.57	1.63	2.33
West Europe	1.94	1.88	1.81	2.01	1.75	1.95	1.79	1.88
East Europe	2.48	2.65	2.56	2.58	2.76	2.62	2.17	2.55
Central Asia	2.54	2.58	2.67	2.67	2.95	2.60	2.30	2.61
South Asia	2.52	2.55	2.65	2.68	2.93	2.57	2.19	2.59
South East Asia	2.46	2.56	2.68	2.71	2.90	2.46	2.19	2.57
China	2.43	2.83	2.81	2.56	2.86	2.36	2.30	2.59
Japan	1.88	2.12	2.27	2.14	2.19	2.02	1.93	2.08
S. Korea	2.30	2.39	2.54	2.55	2.83	2.39	2.63	2.52
Australia	2.07	1.95	1.94	1.99	1.89	2.06	1.58	1.93
Africa	2.65	2.65	2.60	2.79	2.86	2.79	1.89	2.60
Middle East	2.77	2.90	2.70	2.67	3.02	2.56	2.45	2.73
MEAN SCALE SCORES	2.38	2.41	2.4	2.44	2.53	2.38	2.04	

As can be seen in table 10.2, *Italians*, are more comfortable with *Japanese* and less comfortable with people from *Middle Eastern* countries, to hire as 'employees'. As 'residents', *Italians* are likely to most prefer *West Europeans* and least prefer people of *Middle Eastern* origin as 'neighbors'. As 'employees', *Italians* are likely to most prefer a *West European* and least prefer a *Chinese* as their 'boss'. As 'employees' *Italians* are likely to most prefer an *Australian* Company and least prefer an *African* company to work with. *Italians* are most willing to migrate to *West European* destination and least willing to migrate to *the Middle Eastern region*. *Italians* are least likely to be 'partner' in business with *Africans* and most like to be 'partner' with *Western Europeans*. *Italians* are more willing to visit *Australia* and least willing to visit *South Korea* as 'tourists'. It appears that in overall, *Italian* seems to be most comfortable with *West European* cultures and least comfortable *South Korean* cultures.

Table 10.3: Mean comfort scores for respondents from India

INDIA	Q1	Q2	Q3	Q4	Q5	Q6	Q7	Mean
North America	2.15	2.30	2.02	2.00	2.00	2.11	1.70	2.04
Central America	2.43	2.56	2.33	2.35	2.50	2.46	1.91	2.36
South America	2.56	2.59	2.46	2.50	2.54	2.54	1.89	2.44
West Europe	2.02	2.26	2.13	2.15	2.00	2.24	1.65	2.06
East Europe	2.41	2.39	2.30	2.35	2.31	2.39	1.91	2.29
Central Asia	2.35	2.50	2.30	2.44	2.35	2.30	2.00	2.32
South Asia	2.28	2.46	2.31	2.35	2.61	2.44	2.24	2.39
South East Asia	2.30	2.52	2.26	2.35	2.41	2.50	2.00	2.33
China	2.57	2.87	2.89	2.61	3.00	2.65	2.00	2.66
Japan	2.20	2.52	2.24	2.41	2.35	2.31	1.89	2.28
S. Korea	2.48	2.74	2.50	2.61	2.85	2.50	2.89	2.65
Australia	2.63	2.52	2.61	2.50	2.31	2.59	1.70	2.41
Africa	2.83	3.06	3.00	3.00	3.11	2.80	2.11	2.84
Middle East	2.91	2.83	2.94	3.00	3.00	2.94	2.44	2.87
MEAN SCALE SCORES	2.44	2.58	2.45	2.47	2.52	2.48	2.02	

As can be deducted from the table 10.3, as 'employers', *Indians* are most willing to hire *West Europeans* and less willing to hire persons from *Middle Eastern* countries. As 'residents', *Indians* would most prefer *West Europeans* and least prefer people of *African* origin as 'neighbors'. As 'employees', *Indian* would most prefer a *US* 'boss' and least an *African* one. As 'employees', *Indians* would most prefer a *US* company and least an *African* or *Middle Eastern* company. As 'potential migrants', *Indians* will most prefer to move to *the US* or *Western Europe* and least two *African* countries. As 'businessmen', *Indians* would most like to partner with *US* partners and least with *Middle East* partners. *Indians* would most prefer to visit *the US* and least to *South Korea* as 'tourists'. Overall, *the Indians* seem to be most comfortable with *US* and *West Europe* and least with persons from *Middle Eastern* countries.

Table 10.4: Mean 3C scores for respondents from Germany

GERMANY	Q1	Q2	Q3	Q4	Q5	Q6	Q7	Mean
North America	2.37	2.37	2.53	2.39	2.24	2.34	2.00	2.32
Central America	2.68	2.42	2.74	2.39	2.53	2.61	2.21	2.51
South America	2.74	2.63	2.84	2.61	2.71	2.66	2.16	2.62
West Europe	2.21	2.42	2.37	2.26	2.11	2.34	2.00	2.24
East Europe	2.37	2.47	2.42	2.58	2.53	2.34	2.16	2.41
Central Asia	2.74	2.53	2.53	2.50	2.71	2.61	2.29	2.56
South Asia	2.47	2.63	2.71	2.76	2.71	2.53	2.45	2.61
South East Asia	2.37	2.58	2.55	2.61	2.55	2.39	2.21	2.47
China	2.58	2.79	2.84	2.79	2.61	2.63	2.00	2.61
Japan	2.26	2.47	2.50	2.21	2.29	2.34	2.11	2.31
S. Korea	2.68	2.58	2.63	2.61	2.66	2.71	2.89	2.68
Australia	2.47	2.47	2.50	2.39	2.37	2.50	2.11	2.40
Africa	3.00	2.79	3.11	2.79	3.00	2.84	2.05	2.80
Middle East	2.95	2.84	3.00	3.11	3.05	3.00	3.26	3.03
MEAN SCALE SCORES	2.56	2.57	2.66	2.57	2.58	2.56	2.28	

As can be seen from table 10.4, as 'employers', *Germans* are more willing to hire *West Europeans* and less willing to hire persons from *the African region*. *The Germans* would most prefer a *US* 'neighbor' and least someone from *Middle Eastern* origin. As 'employees', *the Germans* would most prefer a *West European* 'boss' and least an *African* one. As 'employees' to work, *the Germans* would most prefer *Western European* company and least prefer a *Middle Eastern* company. As a potential 'migrants', *Germans* will most prefer to move to a *West European* country and least to a *Middle Eastern* country. As 'businessmen', *the Germans* would most like to partner with *West European* or *US* partners and least with *Middle Eastern* partners. *The Germans* would most prefer to visit *US*, *West Europe* or *China* and least to *the Middle East* as 'tourists'. Overall, *the Germans* seem to be most comfortable with *West European* cultures and least with *Middle Eastern* cultures.

Table 10.5: Mean comfort scores for respondents from USA

USA	Q1	Q2	Q3	Q4	Q5	Q6	Q7	Mean
North America	2.38	2.35	2.47	2.41	2.26	2.41	1.88	2.31

Central America	2.68	2.76	3.03	2.91	3.06	2.65	2.09	2.74
South America	2.76	2.65	2.88	2.71	3.00	2.65	2.15	2.68
West Europe	2.38	2.41	2.68	2.44	2.29	2.59	1.74	2.36
East Europe	2.88	2.65	2.88	2.79	2.76	2.71	2.00	2.67
Central Asia	2.91	2.74	2.76	2.74	2.88	2.74	2.15	2.70
South Asia	2.62	2.74	2.97	2.65	2.76	2.74	2.00	2.64
South East Asia	2.62	2.74	2.59	2.65	2.50	2.68	2.00	2.54
China	2.74	2.76	2.91	2.74	2.91	2.79	2.21	2.72
Japan	2.47	2.47	2.50	2.47	2.59	2.44	2.00	2.42
S. Korea	2.59	2.65	2.71	2.59	3.09	2.65	3.00	2.75
Australia	2.68	2.53	2.53	2.59	2.35	2.59	2.09	2.48
Africa	3.03	2.91	2.88	3.00	3.00	3.00	2.21	2.86
Middle East	3.24	2.82	3.00	2.91	3.03	3.00	3.00	3.00
MEAN SCALE SCORES	2.71	2.66	2.77	2.69	2.75	2.69	2.18	

As can be analyzed from above the table, as 'employers', *US* citizens are more willing to hire *West Europeans* or *North Americans* and less willing to hire persons from *Middle Eastern* regions. *US* citizens would most prefer a *US* 'neighbor' and least someone from *African* origin. As 'employees', *US* citizens would most prefer a *US* 'boss' and least a *Middle Eastern* origin 'Boss'. As 'employee' to work, *US* citizens would most prefer *North American* companies and least prefer *African* origin companies. As a potential 'migrants', *US* citizens will most prefer to move to any *North American* country or *West European* country and least to *South Korea*. As 'businessmen', *US* citizens would most like to partner with *North Americans* only and least with *the Middle East* or *African* business 'partners'. *US* citizens would most like to visit *West Europe* and least to *the Middle East* or *South Korea* as 'tourists'. Overall, *US* citizens seem to be most comfortable with *North Americans* and *West Europeans* and least comfortable with *Middle East*.

Table 10.6: Mean comfort scores for respondents from China

CHINA	Q1	Q2	Q3	Q4	Q5	Q6	Q7	Mean
North America	1.90	2.10	1.78	1.75	1.80	1.83	1.60	1.82
Central America	2.23	2.33	2.45	2.20	2.20	2.43	2.00	2.26
South America	2.68	2.45	2.55	2.45	2.55	2.55	2.10	2.48
West Europe	2.00	2.10	2.00	1.95	1.75	2.05	1.65	1.93
East Europe	2.45	2.68	2.43	2.50	2.60	2.55	2.00	2.46
Central Asia	2.45	2.55	2.68	2.45	2.55	2.60	2.10	2.48
South Asia	2.78	2.68	2.73	2.65	2.85	2.80	2.18	2.66

South East Asia	2.68	2.33	2.68	2.45	2.50	2.65	2.00	2.47
China	2.33	2.33	2.35	2.35	2.40	2.35	2.00	2.30
Japan	2.45	2.45	2.30	2.45	2.25	2.35	2.20	2.35
S. Korea	2.68	2.68	2.75	2.70	2.75	2.75	2.20	2.64
Australia	2.55	2.33	2.50	2.35	2.20	2.50	1.90	2.33
Africa	3.00	2.90	2.95	2.90	3.10	2.80	1.90	2.79
Middle East	3.00	2.90	2.90	3.00	3.10	3.00	3.00	2.99
MEAN SCALE SCORES	2.51	2.49	2.50	2.44	2.47	2.52	2.06	

As can be seen in table 10.6, as 'employers', *Chinese* are more willing to hire *US* citizens and less willing to hire persons from *African* and *Middle East* region. *The Chinese* would most prefer a *US* 'neighbor' and least someone from *African* and *Middle East* origin. As 'employees', *the Chinese* would most prefer a *US* 'boss' and least an *African* 'Boss'. As employees, *the Chinese* would mostly prefer *American* companies and would least prefer any *Middle Eastern* company. As a potential 'migrants', *the Chinese* will most prefer to move to any *West European* country and least to *African* or *Middle Eastern* country. As 'businessmen', *the Chinese* would most like to partner with *North Americans* and least with *Middle East* 'partners'. *The Chinese* would most like to visit *North America* and least like to visit *Middle East*, as 'tourists'. Overall, *the Chinese* seem to be most comfortable with *North Americans* and least comfortable with *Middle East*.

Table 10.7: Mean comfort scores for respondents from Saudi Arabia

SAUDI ARABIA	Q1	Q2	Q3	Q4	Q5	Q6	Q7	Mean
North America	2.20	2.20	2.20	2.20	2.11	2.20	2.00	2.16
Central America	2.80	2.20	2.80	2.71	2.60	2.49	2.11	2.53
South America	3.00	2.40	3.00	2.49	2.74	2.74	2.20	2.65
West Europe	1.60	2.20	2.20	2.20	2.20	2.00	2.00	2.06
East Europe	2.40	2.40	2.60	2.40	2.49	2.54	2.14	2.42
Central Asia	2.80	3.00	3.00	3.00	3.00	2.69	2.20	2.81
South Asia	2.00	2.80	2.74	2.66	3.00	2.80	2.20	2.60
South East Asia	2.00	2.60	2.66	2.26	2.26	2.11	2.00	2.27
China	2.60	3.20	2.80	3.00	3.00	2.60	2.20	2.77
Japan	2.20	3.00	2.31	2.20	2.80	2.20	2.00	2.39
S. Korea	2.40	2.80	2.26	2.40	2.80	2.29	2.80	2.53
Australia	2.20	2.40	2.26	2.26	2.20	2.20	2.00	2.22
Africa	3.00	3.20	2.94	3.14	3.00	3.11	2.26	2.95
Middle East	3.20	2.80	2.89	2.80	2.49	2.49	2.71	2.77

MEAN SCALE SCORES	2.46	2.66	2.62	2.55	2.62	2.46	2.20

As can be analyzed from the above table, as 'employers', Saudis are most willing to hire *Western European* citizens and less willing to hire persons from *the Middle East region*. The *Saudis* would most prefer a *US* 'neighbor' and least someone from *African* origin. As 'employee', a Saudi would most prefer a *US* 'boss' and least a *Central Asian* 'Boss'. As 'employees' to work, the *Saudis* would most prefer *American* or *West European* companies and least any *African* company. As potential 'migrants', Saudis will most prefer to move to *North America* and least to *Central Asia, China, South Asia* or any *African* country. As 'businessmen', the *Saudis* would most like to partner with *West European* 'partners' and least with *African* 'partners'. The *Saudis* would most like to visit *North America* or *Western Europe* and least like to visit *South Korea*, as 'tourists'. Overall, *the Saudis* seem to be most comfortable with *West Europeans* and least comfortable with Africa.

Table 10.8: Mean comfort scores for respondents from Pakistan

PAKISTAN	Q1	Q2	Q3	Q4	Q5	Q6	Q7	Mean
North America	2.43	2.43	2.57	2.60	2.46	2.40	2.26	2.45
Central America	3.09	3.14	2.86	3.00	3.09	2.89	2.26	2.90
South America	2.91	2.71	2.57	2.60	2.71	2.80	2.60	2.70
West Europe	2.86	2.43	2.51	2.46	2.29	2.49	2.26	2.47
East Europe	3.00	2.71	2.71	2.80	2.89	2.74	2.00	2.69
Central Asia	2.71	2.86	2.86	2.80	2.94	2.71	2.20	2.73
South Asia	2.14	2.29	2.17	2.23	2.29	2.20	2.40	2.24
South East Asia	2.43	2.43	2.40	2.40	2.34	2.46	2.20	2.38
China	2.29	3.00	3.00	2.66	2.91	2.49	2.89	2.75
Japan	2.71	2.86	2.69	2.86	2.26	2.74	2.26	2.62
S. Korea	3.00	2.57	2.71	2.74	2.89	2.60	3.00	2.79
Australia	2.80	2.86	2.71	2.80	2.46	2.74	2.00	2.62
Africa	3.00	2.71	3.00	3.00	2.86	2.80	2.14	2.79
Middle East	2.91	3.57	2.86	3.09	3.00	3.26	3.00	3.10
MEAN SCALE SCORES	2.73	2.76	2.69	2.72	2.67	2.67	2.39	2.66

As can be seen from the above table, as 'employers', *Pakistanis* are more willing to hire *US* citizens and less willing to hire persons from *East Europe, South Korea* and *African* region. *Pakistanis* would most prefer a *US* or *West European* 'neighbor' and least someone from *Middle Eastern* origin. As 'employee', a *Pakistani* would most prefer a *West European* 'boss' and least a *Chinese* or *African* 'Boss'. As 'employees' to work, *Pakistanis* would most prefer *American* or *West European* companies and least any *Middle Eastern* company. As potential 'migrants', *Pakistanis* will most prefer to move to any *West European* country and least to a *Middle Eastern* country. As 'businessmen', *Pakistanis* would most like to partner with *South Asian* 'partners' and least with *Middle Eastern* 'partners'. *Pakistanis* would most like to visit *West Europe* or *Eastern Europe* and least likely to visit *South Korea* or *Middle East*, as 'tourists'. Overall, *Pakistanis* seem to be most comfortable with *South Asians* and least comfortable with *Middle East*.

Table 10.9: Mean comfort scores for respondents from Nigeria

NIGERIA	Q1	Q2	Q3	Q4	Q5	Q6	Q7	Mean
North America	1.88	2.38	1.75	2.34	1.69	2.00	1.75	1.97
Central America	2.63	3.00	2.75	2.91	3.09	2.81	2.50	2.81
South America	2.50	2.75	2.75	2.59	3.00	2.69	2.19	2.64
West Europe	2.00	2.63	2.50	2.25	2.00	2.25	1.91	2.22
East Europe	2.25	2.50	2.38	2.41	2.44	2.34	2.00	2.33
Central Asia	2.50	2.63	2.75	2.59	2.75	2.59	2.19	2.57
South Asia	2.38	2.63	2.31	2.34	2.59	2.56	2.16	2.42
South East Asia	2.25	2.63	2.34	2.41	2.38	2.50	2.00	2.36
China	2.50	2.88	2.91	2.84	2.75	2.59	2.25	2.67
Japan	2.25	2.63	2.31	2.41	2.00	2.31	2.00	2.27
S. Korea	2.50	3.00	2.91	3.00	2.84	2.59	2.44	2.75
Australia	2.75	2.63	2.69	2.59	2.31	2.66	2.50	2.59
Africa	3.25	3.00	3.16	3.00	3.41	3.19	2.50	3.07
Middle East	2.88	3.00	2.81	2.91	3.09	3.00	2.50	2.88
MEAN SCALE SCORES	2.47	2.74	2.59	2.61	2.60	2.58	2.21	

As can be seen from table 10.9, as 'employers', *Nigerians* are more willing to hire *US* citizens and less willing to hire persons from *the African region*. *Nigerians* would most prefer a *US* 'neighbor' and least someone from *Central American*, *South Korean*, *African* or *Middle Eastern* origin. As 'employees', *Nigerians* would most prefer a *US* 'boss' and least an *African* 'boss'. As 'employees' to work, *Nigerians* would most prefer *American* or *West European* companies and least any *African* or *South Korean* company. As potential 'migrants', *Nigerians* will most prefer to move to *the US* and least to *African* countries. As 'businessmen' *Nigerians* would most like to partner with *US* 'partners' and least with *African* 'partners'. *Nigerians* would most like to visit *the US* and least like to visit *Africa* or *Middle East*, as 'tourists'. Overall, *Nigerians* seem to be most comfortable with *US* and least comfortable with Africa.

Table 10.10: Mean comfort scores for respondents from UK

UK	Q1	Q2	Q3	Q4	Q5	Q6	Q7	Mean
North America	2.09	2.31	2.09	2.20	2.09	2.24	1.84	2.12
Central America	2.60	2.71	2.80	2.64	2.71	2.76	2.51	2.68
South America	2.51	2.60	2.71	2.60	3.00	2.69	2.20	2.62
West Europe	1.89	2.00	2.09	2.04	2.00	1.96	1.80	1.97
East Europe	2.29	2.20	2.40	2.31	2.36	2.36	2.00	2.27
Central Asia	2.71	2.51	2.51	2.60	2.76	2.60	2.20	2.56
South Asia	2.71	2.80	2.71	2.76	2.80	2.78	2.20	2.68
South East Asia	2.80	2.40	2.60	2.49	2.56	2.51	2.09	2.49
China	2.60	2.80	2.91	2.84	2.76	2.60	2.29	2.69
Japan	2.40	2.40	2.31	2.40	2.00	2.42	2.02	2.28
S. Korea	2.40	2.71	2.91	2.60	2.84	2.60	2.44	2.64
Australia	2.20	2.31	2.36	2.40	2.29	2.20	2.00	2.25
Africa	2.80	3.11	3.16	3.00	3.40	3.20	2.51	3.03
Middle East	3.11	3.00	2.80	2.91	3.09	3.00	2.91	2.97
MEAN SCALE SCORES	2.51	2.56	2.60	2.56	2.62	2.57	2.22	

As can be analyzed from table 10.10, as 'employers', *the British* are more willing to hire *Western European* citizens and less willing to hire persons from *the Middle Eastern region*. The British would most prefer a *West European* 'neighbor' and least someone from Africa. As 'employees', *the British* would most prefer a *US* or *West European* 'boss' and least an *African* 'boss'. As employees, *British* would prefer *West European* companies and would avoid an *African* company. As potential 'migrants', *the British* will most prefer to move to *West European* country or *Japan* and least to *African* countries. As 'businessmen', *the British* would most like to partner with *West European* partners and least with *African* partners. *The British* would most like to visit *West Europe* and least like to visit *Middle East*, as 'tourists'. Overall, *the British* seem to be most comfortable with *West European* cultures and least comfortable with *African* cultures.

Table 10.11: Mean comfort scores for respondents from Argentina

ARGENTINA	Q1	Q2	Q3	Q4	Q5	Q6	Q7	Mean
North America	2.00	1.84	2.00	2.00	1.90	1.84	1.71	1.90
Central America	3.03	3.00	2.71	2.74	3.00	2.84	2.61	2.85
South America	3.03	3.29	3.16	3.10	3.16	3.19	2.16	3.01
West Europe	2.13	2.00	2.13	2.00	1.90	2.10	1.81	2.01

East Europe	2.42	2.71	2.71	2.65	2.74	2.71	2.26	2.60
Central Asia	3.00	3.13	3.00	3.00	3.10	3.00	2.45	2.95
South Asia	2.87	3.00	2.97	2.87	3.00	2.90	2.35	2.85
South East Asia	2.71	3.13	2.61	2.65	2.52	2.68	2.26	2.65
China	2.84	3.13	3.00	2.74	3.00	2.81	2.16	2.81
Japan	1.84	1.71	2.00	1.90	1.74	1.84	1.71	1.82
S. Korea	2.16	2.58	2.71	2.61	3.10	2.58	3.06	2.69
Australia	2.00	2.29	2.29	2.32	2.35	2.10	2.00	2.19
Africa	3.42	3.42	3.52	3.45	3.48	3.48	2.48	3.32
Middle East	3.42	3.42	3.61	3.45	3.55	3.48	3.00	3.42
MEAN SCALE SCORES	2.63	2.76	2.74	2.68	2.75	2.68	2.29	

As can be analyzed from table 10.11, as 'employers', *Argentineans* are more willing to hire *Japanese* citizens and less willing to hire persons from *the Middle East* and *African* region. *Argentineans* would most prefer a *US* 'neighbor' and least someone from *the Middle East* or Africa. As 'employees', *Argentineans* would most prefer a *US* or *Japanese* 'boss' and least a *Middle Eastern* 'boss'. As employees, *Argentineans* would prefer *Japanese* companies and would avoid *Middle Eastern* or *African* company. As potential 'migrants', *Argentineans* will most prefer to move to *Japan* and least to *Middle Eastern* countries. As 'businessmen', *Argentineans* would most like to partner with *US* or *Japanese* 'partners' and least with *Middle Eastern* or *African* 'partners'. *Argentineans* would most like to visit *the US* or *Japan* and least like to visit *South Korea*, as 'tourists'. Overall, *Argentineans* seems to be most comfortable with *US* and least comfortable with *Middle East*.

Table 10.12: Mean comfort scores for respondents from Canada

CANADA	Q1	Q2	Q3	Q4	Q5	Q6	Q7	Mean
North America	2.19	2.00	2.41	2.34	2.06	2.19	1.84	2.15
Central America	2.41	2.59	2.81	2.81	2.50	2.75	2.16	2.58
South America	2.22	2.19	2.81	2.69	2.44	2.66	2.09	2.44
West Europe	1.59	2.19	2.41	1.69	1.75	2.00	1.81	1.92
East Europe	2.00	2.19	2.41	2.31	2.34	2.31	2.06	2.23
Central Asia	2.81	2.59	2.81	2.75	2.91	2.75	2.16	2.68
South Asia	2.41	3.19	2.94	3.00	3.09	2.75	2.09	2.78
South East Asia	2.59	3.00	2.66	2.66	2.50	2.69	2.06	2.59
China	2.81	3.19	3.25	3.00	3.00	3.06	2.25	2.94
Japan	2.59	2.19	2.50	2.50	2.59	2.50	2.09	2.42
S. Korea	2.81	3.19	3.00	3.00	3.09	3.00	3.19	3.04

Australia	2.41	2.19	2.34	2.31	2.31	2.41	2.00	2.28
Africa	3.00	3.19	3.16	3.09	3.06	3.16	2.25	2.99
Middle East	3.59	3.41	3.50	3.50	3.56	3.41	3.09	3.44
MEAN SCALE SCORES	2.53	2.66	2.79	2.69	2.66	2.69	2.22	

As can be seen from table 10.12, as 'employers', *Canadians* are most willing to hire *Western European* citizens and less willing to hire persons from *the Middle Eastern region*. *Canadians* would most prefer a *US* 'neighbor' and lest someone from *the Middle East*. As 'employees', *Canadians* would most prefer a *US* or *West European* boss and least a *Middle East* 'boss'. As employees, *Canadians* would most prefer *West European* companies and least any *Middle Eastern* company. As potential 'migrants', *Canadians* will most prefer to move to *West Europe* and least to *Middle Eastern* countries. As 'businessmen', *Canadians* would most like to partner with *West European* 'partners' and least with *Middle East* 'partners'. *Canadians* would most like to visit *West Europe* and least likely to visit *South Korea*, as 'tourists'. Overall, *Canadians* seem to be most comfortable with *Western Europe* and least comfortable with *Middle East*.

Table 10.13: Mean comfort scores for respondents from Japan

JAPAN	Q1	Q2	Q3	Q4	Q5	Q6	Q7	Mean
North America	2.00	2.25	2.75	2.41	2.25	2.16	1.75	2.22
Central America	2.50	2.50	2.75	2.59	2.75	2.66	2.09	2.55
South America	2.75	2.50	2.75	2.59	2.66	2.56	2.06	2.55
West Europe	2.25	2.50	2.50	2.31	2.34	2.41	1.81	2.30
East Europe	2.25	2.00	2.75	2.31	2.44	2.56	2.19	2.36
Central Asia	2.50	2.50	2.75	2.59	2.66	2.69	2.09	2.54
South Asia	2.75	2.50	2.59	2.50	2.66	2.69	2.31	2.57
South East Asia	2.50	2.25	2.31	2.34	2.41	2.53	2.09	2.35
China	2.75	2.75	3.00	2.81	3.09	2.69	2.19	2.75
Japan	2.50	2.50	2.44	2.56	2.53	2.41	2.31	2.46
S. Korea	2.50	2.50	2.56	2.66	2.91	2.56	3.00	2.67
Australia	2.50	2.75	2.66	2.56	2.34	2.66	1.81	2.47
Africa	3.00	3.19	3.16	3.09	3.06	3.16	2.25	2.99
Middle East	3.59	3.41	3.50	3.50	3.56	3.41	3.09	3.44
MEAN SCALE SCORES	2.60	2.58	2.75	2.63	2.69	2.65	2.22	

As can be seen from table 10.13, as 'employers', *Japanese* is most willing to hire *US* citizens and less willing to hire persons from *the Middle East region*.

The Japanese would most prefer a *European* 'neighbor' and least prefer someone from *the Middle East*. As 'employees', *the Japanese* would most prefer a *West European* 'boss' and least a *Middle Eastern* 'boss'. As 'employees' to work, *the Japanese* would most prefer *West European* companies and least any *Middle Eastern* or *African* company. As potential 'migrants', *Japanese* will most prefer to move to *the US* and least to *the Middle East* or *China*. As 'businessmen', *the Japanese* would most like to partner with *US* 'partners' and least with *Middle Eastern* 'partners'. *The Japanese* would most like to visit *the US* and least like to visit *South Korea* and *Middle East*, as 'tourists'. Overall, *the Japanese* seem to be most comfortable with *US* citizens and least comfortable with persons of *Middle Eastern* origins.

Table 10.14: Mean comfort scores for respondents from Portugal

PORTUGAL	Q1	Q2	Q3	Q4	Q5	Q6	Q7	Mean
North America	2.50	2.09	1.75	1.91	2.00	2.09	1.59	1.99
Central America	3.25	2.75	2.75	2.81	2.69	2.75	1.81	2.69
South America	2.59	2.09	3.25	3.00	3.50	3.25	2.00	2.81
West Europe	2.59	2.50	1.75	2.44	2.50	2.44	1.69	2.27
East Europe	2.59	2.25	2.50	2.56	2.75	2.34	2.16	2.45
Central Asia	3.00	3.00	3.00	3.06	3.00	2.94	2.31	2.90
South Asia	2.59	2.66	2.81	2.66	2.69	2.59	2.19	2.60
South East Asia	2.75	3.25	2.75	2.69	2.84	2.44	2.19	2.70
China	3.09	3.16	3.00	3.00	2.66	3.09	2.34	2.91
Japan	1.75	1.50	1.81	1.66	1.69	1.66	1.91	1.71
S. Korea	2.00	2.75	2.50	2.56	2.84	2.41	2.66	2.53
Australia	2.00	2.09	2.31	2.00	2.16	2.09	1.59	2.04
Africa	2.66	2.34	2.75	2.66	3.00	2.56	1.91	2.55
Middle East	3.75	3.50	3.81	3.69	3.75	3.81	2.56	3.55
MEAN SCALE SCORES	2.65	2.57	2.62	2.62	2.72	2.60	2.07	

As can be seen from above table 10.14, as 'employers', *Portuguese* are more willing to hire *US* citizens and less willing to hire persons from *the Middle Eastern region*. *The Portuguese* would most prefer a *European* or *US* 'neighbor' and lest someone from *the Middle East*. As 'employees', *the Portuguese* would most prefer a *Western European* or *US* 'boss' and least a *Middle East* 'boss'. As employees, *the Portuguese* would most prefer *Japanese* companies and would least prefer a *Middle East* company. As potential 'migrants', *Portuguese* will most prefer to move to *North America* and least to *Middle Eastern* countries. As 'businessmen', *the Portuguese* would most like to partner with *US* 'partners' and least with *Middle Eastern* 'partners'. *The Portuguese* would most like to visit *US* and least likely to visit *South Korea*, as 'tourists'. Overall, *Portuguese* seem to be most comfortable with *North American* Countries and least comfortable with *the Middle Eastern region*.

Table 10.15: Mean comfort scores for respondents from Australia

AUSTRALIA	Q1	Q2	Q3	Q4	Q5	Q6	Q7	Mean
North America	2.50	2.38	2.38	2.56	2.25	2.41	2.22	2.38
Central America	2.50	2.25	2.63	2.50	2.75	2.59	2.25	2.50
South America	2.75	2.88	2.88	2.84	3.00	2.84	2.25	2.78
West Europe	2.50	2.63	2.75	2.56	2.28	2.56	2.16	2.49
East Europe	2.75	2.50	2.75	2.59	2.69	2.63	2.25	2.59
Central Asia	2.63	2.75	2.75	2.59	2.84	2.66	2.28	2.64
South Asia	2.63	3.13	2.91	2.72	2.72	2.84	2.25	2.74
South East Asia	2.75	3.00	2.81	2.81	2.66	2.75	2.19	2.71
China	2.63	2.75	2.81	2.84	2.75	2.59	2.31	2.67
Japan	2.75	2.88	2.59	2.63	2.34	2.59	2.09	2.55
S. Korea	2.88	2.75	2.81	2.78	2.84	2.75	2.69	2.79
Australia	2.50	2.38	2.38	2.38	2.09	2.09	2.50	2.33
Africa	3.00	2.88	3.00	2.91	3.09	2.84	2.09	2.83
Middle East	3.00	2.88	3.00	3.00	3.50	2.88	2.69	2.99
MEAN SCALE SCORES	2.70	2.72	2.75	2.69	2.70	2.64	2.30	

As can be seen from table 10.15, as 'employers', *Australians* are most willing to hire *North Americans* or *Western European* citizens and less willing to hire persons from *the Middle East* and *African* region. *Australians* would most prefer a *European* or *North American* 'neighbor' and least someone from *South Asia*. As 'employees', *Australians* would most prefer a *North American* 'boss' and least a *Middle East* or *African* 'boss'. As employees, *Australians* would most prefer *North American* companies and least any *Middle Eastern* company. As potential 'migrants', *Australians* will most prefer to move to *North America* and least to *Middle Eastern* countries. As 'businessmen', *Australians* would like most to partner with *US* 'partners' and least with *Middle East* 'partners'. *Australians* would most like to visit *Japan* and least like to visit *South Korea* and *Middle East*, as 'tourists'. Overall, *Australians* seem to be most comfortable with *North Americans* and least comfortable with persons of *Middle Eastern* origin.

Ranking of respondent countries on their overall country to country CFC levels

Based on the above observations a ranking of the 'destination regions' studied uses two approaches - one based on 'average region wise scores' and second based on 'respondent region score rankings'. The overall 'mean' on culture to culture CFC based on all scales, are tabulated in table 10.16. The final notional overall ranking of the 'destination countries' based on their overall comfort level as analyzed by the study above appears to be as in Table 10.16. As can be seen from the table, there is no major conflict in the overall 3C ranks based on two methods used to calculate them.

Table 10.16: Destination country to country CFC ranks

Country	Rank 1*	Rank 2**
North America	1	1
West Europe	2	2
Japan	3	3
Australia	4	4
East Europe	5	5
South East Asia	6	6
Central America	7	7
South Asia	8	8
South America	9	10
Central Asia	10	9
S. Korea	11	11
China	12	12
Africa	13	13
Middle East	14	14

* Based on average region wise scores. **Based on region ranking scores.

Conclusions:

From the above analysis, it can be concluded that the 'level of intercultural comfort' among different local cultures not only varies from country to country (respondent countries) but also vary from one 'destination country or region' to another. Among the countries studied, it seems there are countries which are more comfortable to foreigners and foreign cultures of specific geographical 'region than others. It may be noted that among the countries studied *Middle Eastern* countries ranks most unfavorably and there could be cultural reasons which makes most respondent cultures comparatively less comfortable in this region. At the same time there is a definite level of CFC of all the respondent countries with destination countries in the *North America* and *West Europe*. A detailed study on specific respondent country and specific destination country and their differences in 'level of culture to culture comfort' may throw more lights on these differences.

It may be noted that the above study is based on a comparatively smaller sample and may be treated as indicative only. However the study gives an insight into the world trends in 'multilateral' intercultural comfort levels among country pairs across the globe. Above study also gives an insight into the nature of such comfort level, 'scale wise'. It should be noted that comfort 'scale' of this study related to the question of choice of region as a tourist destination, indicates quite distinct scores. It appears that this particular variety is most unrelated to other variables describing this phenomenon. A detailed study from a psychological perspective into the choice of respondent country's choice of tourist destination should give new insights into the phenomenon.

Suggested questions for discussion:

1) Why does one culture is more comfortable with another culture, but not so comfortable with another? What explanation could be given to such cultural behavior? Discuss with examples.

2) Discuss the country pair's variation of 'level of CFC' with the *Hofstede's* explanation of reaction of local cultures on arrival of foreigners as discussed in this book.

3) Do you think within intra-country subcultures, there could be a variation in the country pair ' level of CFC', i.e. one subculture may be significantly more comfortable with one destination culture than the other sub culture? Discuss.

4) What explanation can be given to distinctly different responses with respect to a willingness to be a foreign tourist in destination countries in country pair's 'level of CFC' study? Discuss.

Online resources for this chapter, available at:
http://www.vijeshjain.com/books/multinational-workplaces/resources/chapter-10

ANNEXURE

Table 6.1a: CCD questionnaire

PART 1 (General observed variables)	
Short questions	**Full question as used in the questionnaire**
Q1: Unrelated person never getting randomly targeted	There are no insecurities related to the sudden turn of events which may result in an unrelated person getting targeted by the society (where I live in) at large
Q2: Problem may not increase with foreigners	The probability of being branded as accused would not increase if the innocent persons also happen to be foreigners
Q3: Rational Society for foreigners	The society (I live in) remains rational in a situation of major crisis involving those which may apparently look like to have been created by certain groups or persons of certain foreign origin or race
Q4: Religious Society	My native society (read country) is religious
Q5: No Victimization of foreigners based on their religious beliefs	I have never witnessed incidents involving a person of foreign origin persecuted or victimized for his foreign religious belief in my society
Q6: Curious to know other religious thoughts	I was curious to know more about his/her religious beliefs
Q7: No Global problems due to religious beliefs	I do not think there are problems in the modern world which relates to religious beliefs
Q8: Religion not part of	I do not think religion is a part of my daily

186

daily life	life
Q9: No Repulsion with people of other religion	It is not difficult for me to feel close to people who have a different religion from mine
Q10: No existence of a supernatural power	I do not think there exists a supernatural power which may monitor my activities and perhaps influence me in any way
Q11: Belief in the theory of evolution	I believe in the theory of evolution
Q12: No difficulty in understanding of diverse cultures	I never have any difficulty in understanding of diverse national and international cultures
Q13: All cultures have the same status	I do not think there are cultures in the world which may be more superior or more refined than others
Q14: No problem to understand culturally differently	When dealing with culturally different persons I never had difficulty in understanding his or her point of view
Q15: Nothing like my culture represent more values and ethics	I do not think my place's dominant cultures represent more values and ethics than many other cultures of the nation and overseas.
Q16: My culture does not need better recognition	I do not think of the need for my culture getting better recognition in the my country and the world of today to solve many of the problems being faced by the humanity
Q17: Learn from other cultures	I always put efforts to learn from other cultures in one way or another
Q18: Fun to learn about culturally different	Getting to know people from another culture is generally fun for me
Q19: Willing to venture into culturally different	Not like I may never want to move to a new place even if I have better prospects mainly due to the fact that I am unwilling to venture into culturally different
Q20: New ideas coming due to cultural homogenization	Globalization and cultural homogenization have resulted in new ideas and positive cultural influences coming into your country from other countries
Q21: No cultural damage by cultural homogenization	Globalization and cultural homogenization of cultures have not damaged my cultural, economic and religious traditions in many

ways

Q22: No need to stop cultural homogenization	I do not think something should be done to stop such damage
Q23: Can't stop cultural homogenization	Globalization and cultural homogenization of cultures will happen anyway and cannot be stopped
Q24: Enjoy cultural different food	I enjoy eating food of the types originating from other cultures from my country or from overseas.
Q25: Like to visit a culturally different	If I was invited by a culturally different to his house, I will surely follow the invitation
Q26: New learning from visiting a culturally different	If I were invited by a culturally different to visit, it is likely to be a new learning experience for me
Q27: Good feeling to meet a culturally different	I am more likely to feel good to visit a culturally different
Q28: Listen to culturally different music	I often listen to culturally different or overseas music for being different and broadening my view
Q29: Buy culturally different clothing	I like to buy culturally different or foreign clothing brands because I want to keep up with the universal trends in fashion
Q30: Watch culturally different movies	I often watch foreign or culturally different movies because they are windows to different cultures and their ways of life
Q31: Friends must agree with me	I see it's important for me that friends agree with me on most issues
Q32: No problem with a homosexual	I have no issues if someone I know has a homosexual orientation
Q33: No problem with a culturally different boss	I would be comfortable with a colleague from a different culture in a superior position to me
Q34: No problem with a culturally different junior	I would be comfortable with a colleague from a different culture in an inferior position to me
Q35: No problem with a culturally different roommate	I would be comfortable with a roommate from another culture
Q36: Like to see culturally	I would like seeing people from other

different coming to my city	countries or cultures different places of my own country come to my city
Q37: Comfortable with culturally different	I feel comfortable being around culturally different
Q38: Like to have a vacation at cultural different places	If I won a free vacation, I would rather spend it in a different place where I am likely to learn about new cultures and ways of life
Q39: Like to know differences to build friendship	Knowing how a person differs from me may help me build our friendship
Q40: Important to learn other cultures	I think it is important to learn more about other cultures
Q41: Cross cultural interaction should be encouraged	Interacting with people from different cultures should be encouraged because it will help us improve our own values and beliefs
Q42: Immigrants add value	I consider immigration from distant parts of my country and abroad to my city as a value added
Q43: Not like Immigrants getting better salary than us	I do not think Foreigners or culturally different persons living and working in our city are being offered better salaries and more respect than our own people
Q44: Immigrants do not steal jobs	I do not think Foreigners or culturally different persons living and working in our city are stealing away the benefits and privileges from their rightful owners
Q45: Desire to travel in distant places in my country or overseas	Not like I have no desire to travel abroad or distant places in my country
Q46: I find other cultures are similar to us	If I get to know people from other countries and other cultures, I learn that we are more alike than different
Q47: I will be welcome as far off places	Not like I have no desire to travel far off places because I would feel insecure and unwelcome amongst people from a different culture
Q48: Irrational behavior of	In a situation of certain crisis have you

victims blaming a culturally different	witnessed victims behaving irrationally accusing a certain group of persons based on their nationality, region or race?
Q49: Branded accused without proof	Do you think there is a possibility of innocent persons being branded as accused without enough proof in your society
Q50: No encounter with persons preaching their religious beliefs	I have never come across some persons preaching me on his religious orientation

PART 2: (Conditional observed variables)

ST1: Stereotype- Higher Income Group Views

ST1.1: Enterprising Below Income	Below average income persons are generally enterprising enough to look forward to a bright rich future
ST1.2: Below income as Loyal Employees	Below average income persons can generally be trusted as loyal employees
ST1.3: Below income as Trustworthy	Below average income persons can generally be trusted to work given to them for monetary rewards

ST2: Stereotype- Lower Income Group Views

ST2.1: Caring higher income	Above average income persons care about the lower income group
ST2.2: Reliable higher income	Above average income persons can generally be relied on
ST2.3: Helpful higher income	Above average income persons may be willing to help highly needy lower income group persons with money or other resources

ST3: Stereotype-Men's Views

ST3.1: More Chores for women	Women should do more house chores than men
ST3.2: Women more talkative	Women are more talkative and cannot keep an important family secret for long
ST3.3: Women likes to be with women	Women generally like the company of females more than males

ST4: Stereotype- Women's Views

ST4.1: Caring Men	Men generally care enough for the emotions of women

| ST4.2: Loving Men | Men generally love the way women want them to be |
| ST4.3: Respecting Men | Men normally respect women and tend to give the first right of way |

ST5: Stereotype- Situational Discrimination

Have you ever had a problem with a foreigner? If yes answer the following questions

ST5.1: No Problem with someone from my own culture	The problem may not have occurred if the person happened to be a person from my own city and culture
ST5.2: Different behavior with common culture	I would have behaved differently if the person would have been from a common culture
ST5.3: Culturally different should be more careful	Person should have been more careful in dealing with me, because of his/her cultural origin while being in my city
ST5.4: Problem related to his origin	The peculiar behavior of the person was related to his/her cultural origin
ST5.5: Behavior was expected due to his cultural origin	His/her behavior was on expected lines in keeping with his/her specific cultural origin

PART 3: (Demographic Questions - General)

Country of Residence	Present Country of Residence
Region	Geographical Region
City of Residence	Present City of Residence
Age	Age
Residential Status	Residential Status
Education Level	Education Level
Income Group	Income Group

Table 10.1a: Questionnaire used for CFC among country pairs

Question No 1

As an employer if you happen to choose from among a set of candidates with similar skills and requisites, if you will be thinking of their country of origin as a factor of choice, please mention your order of preference. (The following table for answers is used in all the subsequent questions in the questionnaire)

Answers table*	Strongly Yes	Yes	Can't Say	No	Strongly No
North America	☐	☐	☐	☐	☐
Middle America	☐	☐	☐	☐	☐
South America	☐	☐	☐	☐	☐
Europe (West)	☐	☐	☐	☐	☐
Europe (East)	☐	☐	☐	☐	☐
Central Asia	☐	☐	☐	☐	☐
South Asia	☐	☐	☐	☐	☐
South East Asia	☐	☐	☐	☐	☐
China	☐	☐	☐	☐	☐
Japan	☐	☐	☐	☐	☐
Korea	☐	☐	☐	☐	☐
Australia	☐	☐	☐	☐	☐
Africa	☐	☐	☐	☐	☐

Middle East   ⌐   ⌐   ⌐   ⌐   ⌐

Question No 2

As a resident in your city / country, if you happen to choose a new house having neighbor of a foreign origin, is it likely that your choice of housing unit will be influenced by the country of origin of your neighbor. If you will be thinking of their country of origin as a factor of choice, please mention your order of preference.

Question No 3

As an employee if you happen to choose from among a set of job offers with similar potential and remuneration, you may be thinking of the country of origin of your boss. If you will be thinking of their country of origin as a factor of choice, please mention your order of preference.

Question No 4

As an employee if you happen to choose from among a set of multinational company (MNE) with similar prospects to work abroad. If you will be thinking of their country of origin as a factor of choice, please mention your order of preference.

Question No 5

As a potential migrant to a foreign country getting a new job from several choices of countries, you may be thinking of the country as a factor of choice of your new job. If you will be thinking of their country of origin as a factor of choice, please mention your order of preference.

Question No 6

As a businessman, you have to choose a global business partner, you may be thinking of their country of origin as a factor of choice of your business partner. If you will be thinking of their country of origin as a factor of choice, please mention your order of preference

Question No 7

If you would think of spending your holidays in the near future, you would prefer to go which of the following destinations?

(*Note: Same answer table was used for each question as was used n question 1.)

INDEX

ABOUT THE AUTHORS

Dr. Vijesh Jain

Dr. Vijesh Jain is Associate Professor of International Business Management, at *Institute of Technology and Science, India*. He obtained his PhD is from *University of Mysore, Mysore, India*. His topic of PhD research was related to cross cultural management. Having a Masters in International Business from *Indian Institute of Foreign Trade* (IIFT), *New Delhi*, he is a Chemical engineering graduate from *Birla Institute of Technology and Science* (BITS), *Pilani, India*.

He has a corporate experience of more than 17 years and an academic & research experience of 10 years. He has published research papers in *European Journal of Cross-Cultural Competence and Management, International Journal of Business and Management, European Journal of Business and Management* and *Ekonomika Management Inovace*. He is also on the editorial board of several reputed journals, including *Amity Business Review*.

He has also presented several research papers in international conferences including EURAM conference in *Holland* and IAMB conference in *Istanbul, Turkey* and has widely traveled to different countries. He regularly conducts MDPs and workshops for practicing persons as well as for business faculty members. He is also an active consultant.

Dr. Vijesh is also spearheading an international research project related to global understanding of different cultures of the world. As part of his corporate career, *Dr. Vijesh* was actively engaged in international trading functions related to marketing, logistics, distribution and supply chain management in the global context. During these activities, he interacted with business persons from all over the world understanding their lifestyles and cultural ethos.

Dr. Susana Costa e Silva

Dr. Susana Costa e Silva holds a PhD in Marketing from *University College Dublin (Ireland)*. She got her MSc. Economics from *University of Porto (Portugal)*. She is a senior faculty of Marketing at *Catholic University of Portugal (Porto)*, where she is a researcher in the fields of international business, strategic and international marketing, cross cultural studies, expatriates, trust and alliances. She is also visiting professor at *University of Saint Joseph (Macau, China), Escola Superior de Propaganda e Marketing (Brazil)* and the *University of Wroclaw (Poland)*. She has been since 2007 responsible for the MSc. in Marketing at *Catholic University of Portugal (Porto)*.

Dr. Susana authored and co-authored several books and book chapters in International Business, International Marketing and Cooperation, in *Portugal, the UK, Brazil and the USA*. She has also published articles in scientific journals in the fields of international business, international management and international marketing. She was awarded the Best International Marketing paper at the *European International Business Academy* (EIBA) in *Fribourg* (2006).

Dr. Susana has publications in *International Business Review, The Journal of Global Marketing, The Marketing Review*, and *International Review on Public and Nonprofit Marketing*, among others. She is a member and founder of *Portuguese Academy of Marketing*.

She has been engaged in several projects, academic and otherwise, in the fields of internationalization process, international business, international marketing, international cooperation, trust, social marketing, new business models, value creation, etc. She is also active as a consultant.